LEICESTER BUSES

DAVID HARVEY

AMBERLEY

287 (JF 5890)

Front cover, top: The twenty Leyland Titan TD3s delivered in the summer of 1934 were bodied by Metro-Cammell with an early version of their metal-framed straight-profiled body, distinguishable by the radiused front corner of the offside cab window. 287 (JF 5890) waits for its departure time as it stands in front of the Charles Street premises of JW Hemmings, who were printers and stationers specialising in loose-leaf ledgers and account books. This bus is working on the 27 route to Coleman Road via Copdale Road on 17 July 1948, and looks as though it has been recently repainted. It is carrying an advertisement for Kirby & West, Leicester's own independent dairy, which had been established in 1868 and, until recently, were well known for their idiosyncratic rubber-tyred battery electric milk floats. (R. Marshall)

169 (TBC 169)

Front cover, bottom: Metro-Cammell built half of the bodies for the first batch of a dozen Leyland Titan PD3/1s. These were fitted with Orion-style bodies, which were normally regarded as a lightweight construction; however, buses 167 to 172 weighed 8 tons, 4 cwt, making them 5 cwt more than the three Park Royal-bodied PD3/1s and 2.5 cwt more than the Willowbrook examples. All of the Metro-Cammell-bodied buses were delivered during May 1958, and all survived until the early months of 1975. 169 (TBC 169) is unloading passengers at the bus stop on a hot summer's day in 1959. It is working on the 61 route from Nether Hall and is just on the city side of the railway bridge in Uppingham Road, with the railway signal box standing almost on the bridge behind the bus. The destination number blind is displaying 14, as this was the service that was linked to Nether Hall at this time. (R. Marshall)

1 (A71 FRY)

Back cover, top: The worst of all worlds was achieved in the mid-1980s when the newly redeveloped section of Humberstone Gate, between Gallowtree Gate and Charles Street beyond the Haymarket Centre pedestrian bridge, had been closed to all normal traffic. Buses were still using this section of Humberstone Gate as a major city-centre terminal point but were having to negotiate the shoppers, who themselves were unsure of where to walk. The result was confusing for bus drivers and pedestrians alike, and eventually the road was closed for buses. 71 (A71 FRY), a Dennis Dominator DDA 173 with an East Lancs H43/33F body dating from December 1983, is working on the 40 route to Mowmacre Hill on 13 October 1984. Here, it is about to cross the junction with Gallowtree Gate and turn towards the Clock Tower. (A. J. Douglas)

First published 2016

Amberley Publishing
The Hill, Stroud
Gloucestershire, GL5 4EP

www.amberley-books.com

Copyright © David Harvey 2016

The right of David Harvey to be identified as the Author
of this work has been asserted in accordance with the
Copyrights, Designs and Patents Act 1988.

British Library Cataloguing in Publication Data.
A catalogue record for this book is available from the British Library.

ISBN 978 1 4456 4711 1 (print)
ISBN 978 1 4456 4712 8 (ebook)

Typeset in 10pt on 13pt Sabon.
Typesetting and Origination by Amberley Publishing.
Printed in the UK.

Contents

Acknowledgements

The author is grateful to the many photographers acknowledged in the text who have contributed to this volume. I sincerely thank all of those who are still alive for allowing me to use pictures, many of which were taken more than sixty years ago. Thanks are also due to the late Roy Marshall, Bob Mack and Peter Yeomans, who all printed photographs for me many years ago and then generously gave permission for me to use their material. Where the photographer is not known, the photographs are credited to my own collection. The splendid route maps were produced by Roger Smith. Special thanks are due to Peter Newland for overseeing this volume and providing details of routes, locations and dates from his detailed knowledge and notes, and to my wife Diana for her splendid proofreading. Mike Greenwood and the Leicester Transport Heritage Trust also provided access to historical data and photographic material.

The book would not have been possible without the continued encouragement given by Louis Archard and Connor Stait at Amberley Publishing.

Introduction

On 27 August 1901, the Leicester Tramways Company was taken over by Leicester Corporation after the company's lease to operate had expired. The Corporation bought out the company for the large sum of £134,110. Although most of the company's vehicles were tramcars, of which thirty-five were double-deckers and four were single-deckers, there were also thirty horse-drawn buses and, at the time of the takeover, some 375 horses. The first recorded horse-bus service in the city was mentioned in 1863, while, on Christmas Eve 1874, the first horse-tram route commenced operation to the Folly Inn on Belgrave Road using the 4-foot 8.5-inch standard gauge. By 1886, the company was operating five routes along the main roads radiating from the Clock Tower.

The first Leicester Corporation electric tram service was opened to Belgrave and Stoneygate on 18 May 1904 and, by the summer of 1905, there were some thirteen tram routes radiating from the Clock Tower area in the city centre. After receiving two trial open-top fifty-six-seat trams in late 1903, both mounted on Brill 21E 6-foot wheelbase trucks, one bodied by ERTCW and one by Brush, the ERTCW body was adopted for the new tram fleet. The Brush-bodied car was quickly returned to the manufacturer, before being sold to MET in London and becoming their tram 191 in 1904. In 1904, Leicester Corporation received cars 2 to 99, bodied by ERTCW and based on the design of the original car. In 1905, another forty-one trams arrived, of which 101 to 121 were the first top-covered trams in the fleet. By the time the Melton Road route had opened on 8 June 1905, twelve new electric tram routes had opened in a tremendous effort of Edwardian civic pride. Standardising on four-wheel open-top trams, the last new trams were delivered in 1920, by which time 40-hp motors had become the norm. The bodies were built mainly by UEC, although ten trams, 151 to 160, were delivered from Brush, and, in 1920, trams 161 to 166 were built by the Corporation themselves. The tramcar fleet reached its maximum number of tramcars in 1920, with car 178 being the last passenger tram. Eventually, all cars were top-covered by 1929 and re-motored with 40-hp motors. After the First World War, only three more routes were opened, the last being on reserved track along Blackbird Road, which commenced on 22 June 1924, and the Coleman Road route on 31 March 1927.

The first Corporation motor buses, however, did not arrive in the city until 1924, despite the Corporation having ordered three Dodson-bodied Daimler CCs in 1914. These never even arrived in Leicester, presumably having been commandeered by the war department soon after the outbreak of the First World War. From the early 1920s,

Midland Red and various independent operators were running motor-bus services from Leicester to the surrounding towns and villages. The first buses were used to augment the existing tramways, mainly on radial routes, but gradually a fleet of double-deckers expanded, including Tilling-Stevens TS6s and large six-wheel Guy CXs in the 1920s, before various models of Leyland Titan TDs were delivered throughout the mid-1930s. An unusual purchase was nine Northern Counties-bodied AEC Regent 0661s; these were part of an order built for Cardiff Corporation and diverted to Leicester when financial problems in the Welsh capital led to the completed buses being redistributed to the East Midlands. Gradually, the new interwar housing estates were developed, for which buses became the mode of transport of choice. The first tram route to be replaced was that to Melbourne Road on 13 December 1933, while only two routes – the short-lived Coleman Road service and King Richard's Road service – were withdrawn before the outbreak of the Second World War. The real stars of the pre-war bus fleet were the twenty-five impressively large AEC Renown 0664s: nine with Northern Counties bodies and sixteen with Metro-Cammell bodywork designed to look like those built in Wigan.

With the exception of two 'unfrozen' Leyland Titan TD7s, Leicester did not receive any wartime chassis, but the first post-war buses to enter the fleet were semi-utility AEC Regent 0661 IIs, as well as some of Weymann's earliest post-war double-deck bodies, also on the Regent II chassis. An interim batch of Leyland-bodied Leyland Titan PD1s was also delivered during 1946. Leicester placed orders for 160 new vehicles, including AEC Regent IIIs, Daimler CVD6s and Leylands, which started arriving in November 1948. The most numerous of these were sixty-five long-lived Leyland Titan PD2/1s with Leyland bodies, some of which managed almost twenty years' service. These new post-war buses were purchased in order to close down and replace the trams, as well as the pre-war bus fleet. The former was achieved on 9 November 1949 when the Humberstone route was closed, and the latter by 1950. The result of this large influx of buses resulted in the Corporation not requiring any further new buses for most of the next decade.

After trialling several new buses, Leicester placed their first substantial order for new double-deckers. In May 1958, the municipality took delivery of the first of some 117 seventy-four-seat, 30-foot-long Leyland Titan PD3s. These became the standard bus in the city, with the last one being delivered in January 1968. Despite appearing to be an efficiently operated municipality running an apparently traditional-looking bus fleet, with the use of crew-manned front-engined, half-cab vehicles with open-rear platforms in the 1960s and 1970s, Leicester City Transport was involved in several important new developments. They began running one of the first Park & Ride schemes in December 1966 and pioneered the use of VHF radio and CCTV to improve the efficiency of bus services.

At the end of the 1960s, the unavailability of the Leyland Titan PD3 model led to a brief flirtation with the rear-engined Leyland Atlantean PDR1A/1 but, soon, LCT turned to Metro-Cammell, who had developed both a single and double-deck integral vehicle with Scania engines and running units. The former was called the Metro-Scania, while the latter was the Metropolitan. These powerful buses were not without their faults, but Leicester bought thirty-five of the new single-decker model and a further sixty-eight double-deckers.

A change of general manager, with the arrival of Geoffrey Hilditch, brought about the development of a new double-deck rear-engine chassis from Dennis. Mr Hilditch had become increasingly unhappy at Leyland's 'take it or wait until we decide to build it' attitude, and approached Dennis with an outline of a new chassis. Cooperation between Dennis and LCT led to the introduction of the Dennis Dominator in late 1977 and, over the next twelve years, LCT exclusively bought 144 Dominators.

The long-established independent Leicestershire bus and coach operator, Gibson of Barlestone, was taken over in August 1979 and absorbed into the fleet on 8 October 1982, along with a total of thirteen modern Bedford and Leyland coaches, dating from between 1974 and 1981. This allowed LCT, who had previously only ever owned one purpose-built coach, not only to use Gibson's stage-carriage licences – particularly the busy one from Market Bosworth – but also to have available a private-hire fleet. The latter allowed them to operate excursions and participate in the City Flyer consortium, which involved jointly timetabled express work between Dover and Morecambe with several other municipal operators, including those at Burnley and Pendle, and Maidstone.

In 1984, Leicester Corporation Transport was rebranded as Leicester CityBus. The implementation of the 1985 Transport Act on 26 October 1986, and the deregulation of bus services, abolished road-service licensing and allowed for the introduction of competition on local bus services for the first time since the 1930s. To comply with the Transport Act 1985, in 1986, the assets of Leicester CityBus were transferred to a separate legal entity. In Leicester, competition from other operators, especially Midland Fox, led to the introduction of minibuses, with the fleet of vehicles being branded as Little CityBuses. The gradual decline in revenue and consequent investment led to Leicester City Council selling its 94 per cent shareholding in Leicester CityBus. The undertaking was sold in November 1993 to Grampian Regional Transport Group, who later merged with Badgerline to form FirstBus on 15 June 1995. This resulted in the Leicester operation being rebranded as First Leicester, who continue to be a major operator in the city and who are the direct descendants of the original Leicester Tramways.

Leicester General Managers	Bus garages
A. F. Lucas 1901–1928	Abbey Park Road
H. Pool 1928–1936	Bread Street
B. England 1936–1939	Rutland Street
C. H. Stafford 1939–1950	
J. Cooper 1951–1966	
L. H. Smith 1966–1975	
G. G. Hilditch 1975–1984	
R. Hind 1984–1986	

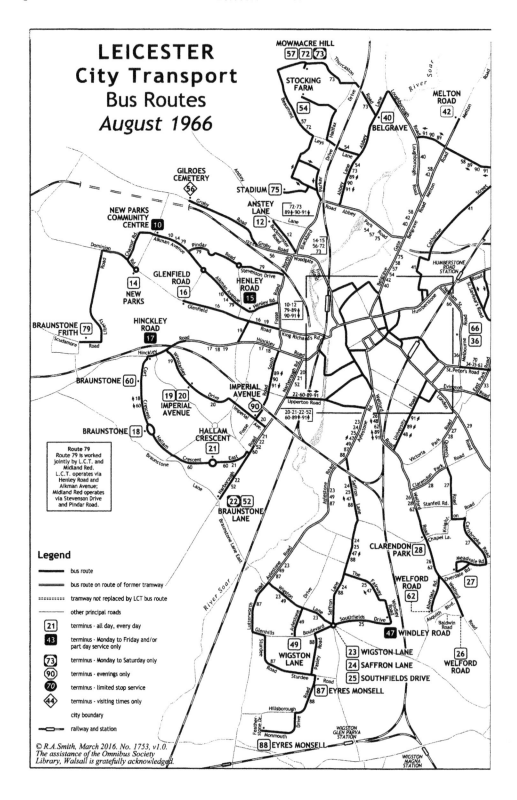

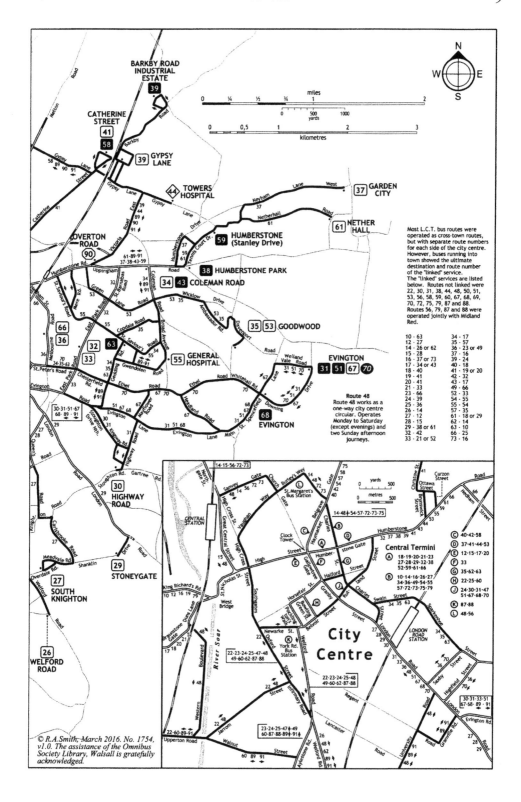

Most L.C.T. bus routes were operated as cross-town routes, but with separate route numbers for each side of the city centre. However, buses running into town showed the ultimate destination and route number of the "linked" service. The "linked" services are listed below. Routes not linked were 22, 30, 31, 38, 44, 48, 50, 51, 53, 56, 58, 59, 60, 67, 68, 69, 70, 72, 75, 79, 87 and 88. Routes 56, 79, 87 and 88 were operated jointly with Midland Red.

10 - 63	34 - 17
12 - 27	35 - 57
14 - 26 or 62	36 - 23 or 49
15 - 28	37 - 16
16 - 37 or 73	39 - 24
17 - 34 or 43	40 - 18
18 - 40	41 - 19 or 20
19 - 41	42 - 32
20 - 41	43 - 17
21 - 33	49 - 66
23 - 66	52 - 33
24 - 39	54 - 55
25 - 36	55 - 54
26 - 14	57 - 35
27 - 12	61 - 18 or 29
28 - 15	62 - 14
29 - 38 or 61	63 - 10
32 - 42	66 - 25
33 - 21 or 52	73 - 16

Route 48
Route 48 works as a one-way city centre circular. Operates Monday to Saturday (except evenings) and two Sunday afternoon journeys.

Central Termini

Ⓐ 18·19·20·21·23 27·28·29·32·38 52·59·61·66
Ⓑ 10·14·16·26·27 34·36·49·54·55 57·72·73·75·79
Ⓒ 40·42·58
Ⓓ 37·41·44·53
Ⓔ 12·15·17·20
Ⓕ 33
Ⓖ 35·62·63
Ⓗ 22·25·60
Ⓙ 24·30·31·47 51·67·68·70
Ⓚ 87·88
Ⓛ 48·56

© R.A.Smith, March 2016. No. 1754, v1.0. The assistance of the Omnibus Society Library, Walsall is gratefully acknowledged.

1924–1930: The Early Bus Fleet

1 (BC 9162), 3 (BC 9164)

The Corporation's first motorbuses were six Brush-bodied Tilling-Stevens TS6s, which had a B32R layout. They all entered service in July 1924. 1 (BC 9164) and 3 (BC 9162), with their large, distinctively styled radiators, stand at the entrance to the garage in 1929. Authorisation for them to be re-bodied as double-deckers had been given on 20 May 1927. This was because, in their original single-decker form, their capacity was insufficient. The new Brush bodies had a H24/26RO seating layout and, by March 1928, had re-entered service in their new guise. The new bodies were top-covered, but had outside rear staircases and a style that looked backwards to designs of the early post-First World War, rather than one with a hint of modernity. The crowds outside Abbey Park Road Garage await the buses leaving the garage in July 1929 on the occasion of the opening of the new bus workshops. All the Tilling-Stevens TS6s were taken out of service in July 1934. (LTHT)

2 (BC 9163)

The first six buses were Tilling-Stevens TS6s, which for three years ran with Brush single-deck B32R bodywork. After three years, these original six buses were re-bodied with Brush H26/24RO double-decker bodywork. These were similar in style to the contemporary bodywork supplied to Birmingham on AEC 504 chassis. One of these original buses, 2 (BC 9163), is parked on the left in its original single-decker form, along with a group of Tilling-Stevens TS6 double-deckers delivered in September and October 1925 including 13 (RY 1578). The buses are in Abbey Road bus garage, soon after its opening on 16 September 1926. All the TS6s were put onto pneumatic tyres from October 1928 and, until the summer of 1927, were the only motorbuses in the City of Leicester Tramways department fleet. This was still dominated by the 178 tramcars, although the writing was beginning to be put on the wall for the trams; no new tram had been introduced into the fleet after 1920 and the last new tram route was opened to Colman Road on 31 March 1927. (LTHT)

4 (BC 9165)

The first buses to be delivered were six Tilling-Stevens TS6s with petrol-electric transmission. The TS6 chassis cost £1,072 10s while the Brush Engineering bodies, built locally at Loughborough, were £536 each. The bodywork had the luxury of having the driver's cab totally enclosed, which was still quite a new feature on half-cab bus bodies. They were ordered so as to operate the first motorbus service from Charles Street to St Philip's Church, Evington, which began on 24 July 1924 and covered a distance of 1.96 miles. Two Corporation employees pose alongside the front of the bus soon after it had been delivered. The high chassis frame necessitated the intrepid passengers to negotiate the four steep steps at the rear of the body. These single-deckers, including bus 4, always ran on rubber tyres, and were only converted to pneumatics after they were re-bodied as double-deckers by Brush. They remained in service until the summer of 1934 when they, along with all the other Tilling-Stevens TS6 buses, were replaced by a batch of twenty Metro-Cammell-bodied Leyland Titan TD3s. (LTHT/R. Marshall Collection)

6 (BC 9167)

In their original single-decker guise, the first six City of Leicester Tramways department Tilling-Stevens TS6 looked very similar to countless other single-deckers of the period, which were built for municipalities and companies across the United Kingdom. Parked at the Brush works in Loughborough, the bodywork still had echoes of turn-of-the-century tramcar bodies. The TS6 sported a high frame and a 5722cc pair-cast, four-cylinder petrol engine rated at 40 hp, which was coupled to a series-wound motor joined to an overhead worm rear axle by a cardan shaft. This gearless transmission made the TSM chassis comparatively easy to drive, but was more difficult to maintain than gearbox transmissions and a conventional clutch. The advantage of this was that Tiling-Stevens buses were never commandeered by the War Department, unlike buses throughout the country that were fitted with a conventional clutch and gearbox. (Brush)

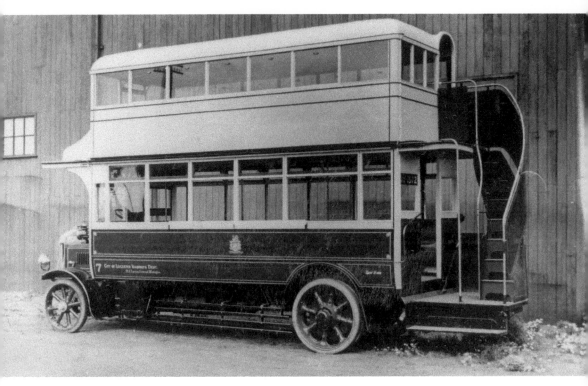

7 (RY 1572)

Posed in the shadow of the Brush coach-building factory in Loughborough during September 1925 is 7 (RY 1572). This Tilling-Stevens TS6 petrol-electric bus had a totally enclosed H26/24RO body, with an outside staircase of a style that was pioneered by the Brush Company, although it was more usual on an AEC 504 chassis. There was still evidence of the tramcar origins of the bodywork. RY 1572 was used to operate a new bus route from Welford Place to Aylestone Recreation Ground, which was instigated on 5 October 1925. Its double-decker capacity proved to be most useful, seating only six fewer than the contemporary four-wheel Leicester tramcar. (Brush)

10 (RY 1575)

Under repair in Abbey Park Road Garage over the pits in 1927 is 10 (RY 1575). This bus was one of the eight Brush-bodied Tilling-Stevens TS6s built as double-deckers with Brush H26/24RO bodywork. The bus has had its Tilling-Stevens 5722cc pair-cast, four-cylinder petrol engine removed for repair. The garage itself dated from the opening of the electric tram services in 1904, when it was the main depot, housing the original 99 tramcars ordered for the city. By September 1926, a large garage was constructed next to the tram sheds to house the city's growing motorbus fleet; this garage was doubled in size in 1934 with another extension to cater for even more motorbuses. On the right is one of the two Leyland Tower Wagons, built in either 1923 or 1924. (LTHT)

11 (RY 1576)
Standing on the forecourt of Abbey Park Road Garage is 11 (RY 1576). The bus appears to be brand new, judging by the patina on the paintwork, and this suggests that it was photographed in October 1925. It is a Tilling-Stevens TS6, whose transmission system was beginning to be phased out in favour of crash gearboxes. It was, perhaps, slightly surprising that Leicester purchased this somewhat antiquated and complex chassis. Although the Brush H26/24RO body, with its enclosed cab and covered upper saloon, was about as up to date as the mid-1920s PSV legislation would allow, it was still rather old fashioned as far as the travelling public were concerned. (LTHT/D. M. Bailey Collection)

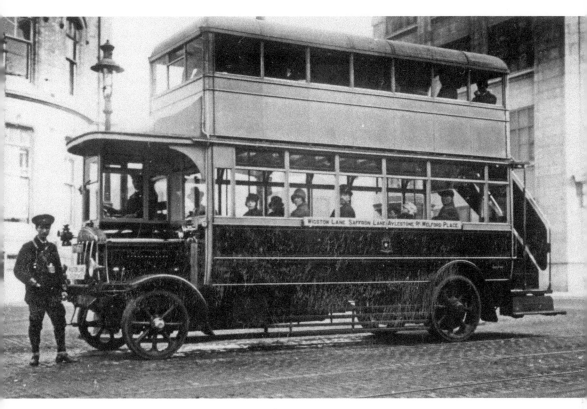

12 (RY 1577)

12 (RY 1577) was a 1925 Tilling-Stevens TS6 petrol-electric, with a Brush H24/26RO outside-staircase body, and stands here in Welford Place across the front of Pocklington's Walk on Monday 22 March 1926. The bus, in original condition on rubber tyres, is about to journey to Wigston Lane via Aylestone Road and Saffron Lane in order to serve the large area around the Saffron Lane housing developments to the south of the city. The driver of bus 12 is already in the cab, while the conductor, with his Brecknell, Munro & Rogers ticket machine, poses for posterity in front of his bus. The passengers are all looking at the cameraman with a certain curiosity. This bus would remain in service until 1934 (on pneumatic tyres for the final four years), when it would be sold to J. Stockwell, a showman, during the July of that year. (J. Cooper)

14 (RY 1579)

Above: 14 (RY 1579) was sold to a showman in July 1934 and has only just arrived with its new owner. Not only is it still displaying its fleet number and the name of its former legal owner, but it is also on pneumatic tyres. Photographs of these Brush-bodied Tilling-Stevens TS6 buses with pneumatic tyres are rare, despite the buses numbered 1 to 14 operating on them since 1929. The new tyres helped to considerably alter and modernise the appearance of these buses. The wife of the showman poses in the cab of their newly acquired bus, while his daughter sits atop the radiator. One can almost hear the woman saying to her husband, 'Can I sit in the cab, m'duck?' (*Leicester Evening Mail*/A. P. Newland)

15 (RY 4373)

Opposite above: The Guy B was a normal-control, straight-framed, 2.5-ton bus chassis, intended for a maximum of twenty-six passengers. It had been introduced in 1919 and, after 1926, was equipped with a Guy four-cylinder, 4.58-litre petrol engine. The first four were supplied to Leicester in July 1927, and were numbered 15–18. These useful little buses weighed a fraction over 4 tons and had forward-entrance bodies built by Brush in nearby Loughborough. They seated twenty-five passengers and were bought for the Marfitt Street and Overton Road service. It is standing on the forecourt of Abbey Park Road Garage when new in the summer of 1927. (J.Cooper)

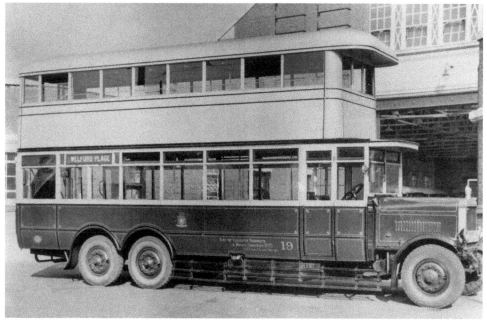

19 (RY 4377)

Above: The sheer size of the Guy C six-wheel chassis is easily seen as 19 (RY 4377), the first of the twenty-three-strong Leicester fleet, stands posed in front of the bus garage at Abbey Park Road. Only forty-nine CXs were built, with Leicester having the largest number and Wolverhampton having nineteen. Weighing in at 6 tons, 13.5 cwt, these 29-foot-long buses were bodied by Brush but, with their enclosed rear platforms and a straight staircase, they had a capacity of thirty passengers in the upper saloon and only twenty-six downstairs. The CX must have been a challenge for the Leicester bus drivers, who were used to the Tilling-Stevens TS6 petrol-electric chassis, as the Guys had a right-hand-mounted gated four-speed gearbox and a cone clutch, which gave a start from stationary to 5 miles an hour in a half-second-long forward lurch. (LTHT)

23 (RY 5544)

Standing in Welford Place in front of the Victorian-built offices on 14 September 1928 is 23 (RY 5544). This bus is being used on the service to Wigston Lane, which will leave the city by way of Aylestone Road. It is a Guy CX with a Guy 7.69-litre petrol engine, which was enclosed underneath the long bonnet. The buses only achieved a little over 4 mpg in service. These Guy behemoths were some of the last normal-control double-deckers to enter service in the United Kingdom as, within months of being delivered in January 1928, this type of bus was made obsolete by the introduction of the low-framed, two-axled Leyland Titan TD1. The fifty-six-seater body was built by Brush with, advantageously, a totally enclosed rear platform and staircase. (J. Cooper)

24 (RY 5545)
Travelling towards the city centre near to the tram terminus in Narborough Road is 24 (RY 5545). It is operating on the newly introduced bus service from Coalpit Lane to the 1920s housing estates, which were being built towards the Narborough Road city boundary beyond the tram terminus. This was at the time when the Corporation policy was to maintain the existing tram service but use buses to serve the new housing estates beyond the old tram termini. Behind the bus is a Corporation tramcar working on the main Narborough Road service. 24 is one of the seven six-wheeled normal-control Guy CXs that entered service in January 1928. They were all were fitted with Brush H30/26R bodywork, with generously spaced seating. (A. P. Newland Collection)

33 (RY 5554)

Above: Standing at the entrance to Abbey Park Road Garage in later life is 33 (RY 5554). This was one of eleven normal-control Guy B single-deckers. The Brush B25F bodywork had a pronounced tumblehome at the bottom of the side and rear panels, giving the bus an even greater vintage appearance, that of a style produced in the early 1920s. 33 entered service in December 1927 and was usually operated as a driver-only bus, as vehicles with a capacity of fewer than twenty-six were allowed, under the legislation of the time, to be without a conductor. 33 was one of the last five Guy B types to remain in service; it was withdrawn on 30 June 1939 and converted into an ambulance in August 1939, before being transferred to the Auxiliary Fire Service in June 1940. This official photograph was taken in 1937 in order to plan where advertisements would be placed on the Corporation buses. Needless to say, the rear panels were extensively used for this revenue-making scheme. (LTHT)

36 (RY 6471)

Opposite above: Twelve years after being formed, Leicester Tigers moved in 1892 to their present ground at Welford Road, Leicester. Judging by the number of women in the crowd, it was the Tigers who were playing at home rather than Leicester City FC at the nearby Filbert Street. The totally enclosed City of Leicester tramcar 64 was working on a football-special service at the Welford Road–Aylestone Road junction in about 1935. This tram was originally built as an open-topper in 1904 by ERTCW; it was top-covered and given a vestibule in 1925, with the upper saloon assembly being supplied by UEC. There are no less than five Brush-bodied Guy CXs visible, of which 36 (RY 6471) is on the left, while the very last one, 52 (RY 7859), is partly hidden by the tram (Leicester Evening Mail)

44 (RY 7851)

Above: An unidentified Brush-bodied Karrier JK four-wheel demonstrator leads 44 (RY 7851) out of Abbey Park Road Garage. 41 is the first of the trio of Guy Bs bought by the Corporation, and entered service in Leicester on 29 June 1929. They had Guy 4.58-litre four-cylinder petrol engines, driving a four-speed gearbox through a cone clutch, and Guy's own B25F bodywork. The buses had a seating capacity small enough to be able to be operated as one-man vehicles, and were used mainly on the Marfitt and Overton Road services. These normal-control Brush-bodied single-deck buses were similar to buses supplied about the same time to Burton Corporation. 44 was one of the last three of the normal-control Guy Bs supplied to Leicester. Behind the single-deckers in the gloom of Abbey Park Road Garage are a trio of Brush-bodied Tilling-Stevens TS6s petrol-electric double-decker buses. (LTHT/D. R. Harvey Collection)

48 (RY 7855)

Above: Appearing as if it has not been used for some time, 48 (RY 7855), by now numbered 248, stands in Abbey Park Road Garage yard in about 1942, shortly before it was withdrawn from service. Had the intended closure of the Leicester tram system not been postponed because of the outbreak of the Second World War, all the Guy CXs would have probably survived for a little longer. However, with a surfeit of trams, there was little need for them to stay in service – although 48 was one of five of these buses to last into 1942. The bus entered service on 2 August 1929 and this batch, from 47 to 52, was the last of these six-wheeled normal-control Guy CX models to be built as double-deckers. The Brush H30/26R body did have an enclosed rear platform and staircase, as well as having cantrail panels in the lower saloon rather than tram-style windows, but still managed to look old-fashioned. 248 is fitted with wartime headlight masks and has white painted wing edges. (R. Marshall Collection)

48 (RY 7855)

Opposite above: Brush-bodied Guy CX 48 (RY 7855) was renumbered as 248 in 1937. It remained in service until 1942, mainly for use in the peak periods, but was kept in stock until after the end of the Second World War. It was then sold to a showman on 12 September 1945, but was not recorded with them until April 1946. It was quickly cut down to a single-decker for use as a storage lorry for fairground equipment. In this form, it looked a very impressive vehicle, especially with its lined-out panelling. RY 7855 was still being used as a showman's lorry in Nottingham on Sunday 13 October 1957, but disappeared off the fairground circuit soon afterwards. (R. Butler)

49 (RY 7856)

Above: Parked in Abbey Park Road Garage yard in 1937 is 49 (RY 7856). This was one of the large six-wheel normal-control Guy CXs fitted with a Guy 7.69-litre petrol engine. 49 entered service on 2 August 1929, and had a Brush H30/26R body, weighing 6 tons, 13.5 cwt unladen. Although the bus had two steep steps into the lower saloon, this did enable the floor to be flat throughout its not-inconsiderable length. The bus has an unmissable advertisement for 'Butler's Fever & Flu Powders', a long-forgotten cold cure. 49 was one of the last of five Guy CXs to remain in service, and lasted until mid-1942. (LTHT)

VC 1778

Above: The two-axle Maudslay Mentor ML7BC chassis had a much lower and more modern chassis. Most were bodied as single-deckers, although a few were double-deckers, including a trio for nearby Coventry City Transport. VC 1778 was the only ML7 demonstrator, and was bodied by Hall Lewis with a modern fifty-seat, low-height double-decker with an enclosed staircase. The chassis design enabled the bodywork to get as low as only 13 feet but the design, although quite liked by the traffic department, was hampered by the disappointing performance of the six-cylinder petrol engine. The bus is demonstrating at the MT Conference in 1929. The bus was sold to S. Toone of Billesdon and received an early Barton-style Willowbrook H26/24F body in November 1936. (A. Ingram)

OU 4028

Above: A Strachan-bodied Thornycroft BC was demonstrated to Leicester at the beginning of June 1930. Little is known about this bus, save for it having an 85-bhp Thornycroft petrol engine and that it was registered OU 4028 in Hampshire by Thornycroft. It was in Leicester from 17 May 1930 until 8 June 1930 before returning to Thornycroft in Basingstoke on 11 June. City of Leicester Tramways department was not impressed and did not place an order for either the chassis type or the body manufacturer's order book. The bus is standing outside the London & Scottish Assurance offices in Welford Place when working on the Uplands Road service on 1 June 1930. (J. Cooper)

UK 7456

Opposite below: The six-wheeled Sunbeam Sikh K101 was an attempt by another failing car manufacturer to break into the bus-and-coach industry at the end of the 1920s. Only three Sikh chassis were built, the first being converted to the prototype MS1 Weymann-bodied trolleybus, JW 526. The third chassis was bodied in 1932, when it was sold to Westminster, a London independent. This, the second chassis, had a Sunbeam 7.982-litre petrol engine, was registered (UK 7456), and had a more varied career as the Wolverhampton company's demonstrator. It was exhibited at the 1930 Olympia Show in London, and was used by Leicester in May 1930 when already ten months old. UK 7456 was demonstrated to Birmingham Corporation between 5 November and 1 December 1930, as well as being hired by Wolverhampton Corporation and Mansfield District in 1931. The six-bay Dodson H35/32R body on the Sikh chassis looks quite impressive, as UK 7456 demonstrates on Leicester Corporation's Norwood Road 11 service in Highfield Street on 10 May 1930. It was not surprising, perhaps, that it was not a success in Leicester, bearing in mind that it also operated in its home town of Wolverhampton and even there it failed to impress! It finally found a home with Derby Corporation in 1933. (J. Cooper)

JF 223

Some provincial municipalities were attracted by the current LGOC ST body design built by Ransomes, Simms & Jefferies with a more modern-looking square front cab. Two RSJ bodies were built for West Bridgford UDC and six for Exeter Corporation, while a demonstrator went to Leicester Corporation in their livery, registered JF 223 and used during the early summer of 1930. Looking very smart, it is parked in Humberstone Gate in about April 1930. The forty-nine-seater body had the unusual features of being equipped with full-drop lower-deck windows and sliding windows upstairs; it also had a straight staircase and was slightly lower than most provincial centre-gangway double-deckers. It also had an early version of the 7.4-litre six-cylinder petrol engine. JF 223 was not purchased by Leicester, eventually becoming Barton Transport 248 in 1936. (J. Cooper)

1931–1936: The First Pre-War Standard Bus Fleet

53 (JF 1529)

During 1931, several operators, mainly municipalities, placed single trial oil-engined Regents in service. These had the newly introduced AEC-Acro 8.1-litre engine. This rather long engine was accommodated in the engine bay by the simple expedient of mounting the radiator as far forward as possible, resulting in a 'snout-like' appearance. Chassis 6611156 was supplied to City of Leicester Tramways and Motor Omnibus department in June 1931, and was registered JF 1529. The bus had Brush bodywork, with a sloping piano-front style that was a variation of the Loughborough-based coachbuilder's recently developed design. This body style was also Leicester's contemporary standard, being supplied on both Leyland Titan TD1 and TD2 chassis in 1931 and 1932. 53's body had a straight staircase, resulting in it accommodating only twenty passengers in the lower saloon. Unusually it had a spare tyre mounted below the rear platform window, behind the normal panelling. As 253, it remained in service until June 1949. It is parked in Wyvern Avenue while working on the 27 service to Humberstone Gate towards the end of its long life in 1947. (D. R. Harvey Collection)

54 (JF 1530)

54 (JF 1530) was used by Brush as the vehicle for their official photographs. This bus was new in June 1931, and was the first of a batch of four buses numbered 54 to 57. These were Leicester's first modern four-wheeled double-deckers but, although their low-frame Leyland Titan TD1 chassis revolutionised double-deck bus design only three years earlier, the Brush H26/24R body design looked tall and gaunt with a vestigial piano-front between the decks. Even when new, it was beginning to look somewhat dated. Having served with London Transport between 27 October 1940 and 20 April 1941, the bus was returned to service by LCT and eventually withdrawn on 25 February 1947, along with 55 and 56. (Brush)

57 (JF 1533)

Passing a branch of Sketchley's Dry Cleaners on 18 August 1931 is 57 (JF 1533), a Brush-bodied Leyland Titan TD1, two months after it had entered service. 57 has just passed the junction at Campbell Street, where Charles Street joins London Road. The buildings on the corner of Campbell Street have recently been demolished. As it passes over the tram tracks, it is approaching London Road railway station. Bus 57 will then climb the steep hill in London Road, lined with large Victorian villas, before turning left into Evington Road on its way to the new housing estates being developed in the valley of Evington Brook. It would remain in service until 9 March 1946, after which it would also be sold to Barton of Chilwell. (Leyland Motors/M. Sutcliffe Collection)

60 (JF 2707)

Above: For many years, the focal point of London Road has been the railway station. The first station on the site was opened on 5 May 1840 by the Midland Counties Railway as a part of their line linking Derby, Nottingham, Leicester and Rugby. The MR rebuilt the station between 1892 and 1894 to a design by the architect Charles Trubshaw, who gave the new station the impressive frontage on London Road. This features four entrance archways, with the city-end pair being inscribed 'Departure' and the southern pair each carrying the carved word 'Arrival'. Passing the main entrance to the station is a large 7-ton Leyland four-wheel lorry, towing an equally impressive trailer followed by a Morris Ten dating from around 1934. Behind it is Leicester bus 60 (JF 2707), one of the six Brush-bodied Leyland Titan TD2s dating from May 1932. In the middle of the road, also travelling away from the city centre, is UEC-bodied tram 147, dating from 1913 and mounted on the usual Leicester standard Brill 21E 6 foot-long trucks. The bus on the left is 64 (JF 5006), a 1933 Leyland Titan TD3 with a MCCW H26/24R body. (*Leicester Evening Mail*)

59 (JF 2706)

Opposite: Parked in front of Abbey Park Road Garage in 1937, and sporting a very bald offside front tyre is 59 (JF 2706). This was the second of the six Leyland Titan TD2s delivered in May 1932. They had H26/24R bodies built by Brush, which were very similar to the bodies supplied eleven months earlier on the Leyland Titan TD1s. The bus was photographed to assess the positioning of the advertisements, which were being introduced on the bus fleet in the mid-1930s. 59 was one of the five Leicester buses sent to London on 27 October 1940 and, on its return, it re-entered service until it was replaced by one of the AEC Regent IIs of 1946. (LTHT)

61 (JF 2708)

Above: Looking a bit tired and down-at-heel, 61 (JF 2708), renumbered as 261 in 1937, stands in Charles Street in 1944. Behind the bus at the unusually numbered 47½ Humberstone Gate are the premises of S. H. Shaw & Son, who were butchers. The shop was on the corner of Charles Street. The bus is a Brush-bodied Leyland Titan TD2 with a 7.6-litre Leyland petrol engine and a fully floating rear axle, distinguishable from the earlier TD1 by having a large flat-faced rear axle hub case. 61 is in full wartime garb, with masked headlight and white edging paint. The lady conductor stands under the canvas awning of Mrs Wainwright's shop in Charles Street. (R. Marshall Collection)

63 (JF 2710)

Above: It's wash day in Abbey Park Road Garage! In the days before automatic bus washes, the cleaning of buses was quite labour intensive, not to mention a wet and tiring job. There would be at least one man on the hose and one with a long brush, and it would take ten to fifteen minutes to get the bus spotless. The nearside profile of the two buses in the garage washing area shows that the six-bay piano-front Brush bodywork on 63 (JF 2710), a Leyland Titan TD2 delivered in May 1932, looks quite dated when compared to the Metro-Cammell five-bay body on Leyland Titan TD3 66, (JF 5008), which is only two years newer. 63 remained in service until March 1946, renumbered as 263, and was one of five of these 1932-vintage TD2s to be sold to Barton Transport of Chilwell as their 461. (LTHT)

262 (JF 2709)

Opposite below: Some 475 buses were sent to London immediately after the Blitz began in the capital in October 1940. The prospect of the destruction of many of London's buses in air raids resulted in the Ministry of Transport and the regional Traffic Commissioners securing the loan buses from the rest of the country. This was something of a false move, as the numbers of buses destroyed proved to be tiny when compared to the government's estimates, and, by the spring of 1941, LPTB were sending buses back into the provinces to replace air-raid-damaged vehicle stock in their 'home' bus fleets. On 27 October 1940, five of the Brush-bodied Leyland Titan TD2s were sent to London, including 262 (JF 2709). It has the route number 15 chalked on the blacked-out platform window as it approaches Trafalgar Square on the Ladbrooke Grove–East Ham (White Horse) service, operated by Upton Park Garage. (A. D. Packer)

64 (JF 5006)

Above: On 12 March 1944, the first of the five 'modern-looking' double-deckers owned by City of Leicester Tramways was Metro-Cammell-bodied Leyland Titan TD3 64 (JF 5006), by now numbered 264. It is working on the 22 service along Narborough Road to Braunstone Lane as it passes the offices of the Leicester Permanent Building Society; it is well laden and down on its rear springs. 264 was the last to be repainted in the earlier cream livery in early 1937; it still has the well-worn traces of wartime white paint on the edges of the mudguards, and headlight masks, which were of little use to the driver at night in the blackout. The MCCW-bodied bus was delivered in December 1933, and traces of this design, with its sloping and curved front panels, lingered on until the very early 1950s. (W. J. Haynes)

67 (JF 5009)

Opposite below: On 17 July 1948, Leyland Titan TD3 267 (JF 5009) passes the Rendezvous Café in Humberstone Gate. Behind the bus, the impressively tall, first-rounded windows are part of the Palais de Danse night spot, with a British-built Ford Tudor V8 saloon mounted on very large tyres and a sleek-looking Riley 1.5-litre Kestrel saloon in front of it. The Metro-Cammell-bodied fifty-seater is working on the 26 route to Melbourne Road, but is working empty in order to turn round and gain its stop on the other side of Humberstone Gate. It is noticeable that the tram track and overhead remain in use for the Humberstone and East Park services. (R. Marshall Collection)

266 (JF 5008)

Above: Parked on the garage forecourt at Abbey Park Road on 20 November 1940 is bomb-blasted 266 (JF 5008), one of the 1933 batch of five Leyland Titan TD3s. Despite having nearly all its saloon windows blown out, part of the roof removed and most of the ceilings brought down, the metal-framed Metro-Cammell body work is still structurally sound. 266 was working to Catherine Street when a bomb landed at the Saxby Street and Sparkenhoe Street junction, demolishing all the buildings on all four corners of the crossroads. Thirteen people were killed, and another thirteen were seriously injured. 266 was subsequently rebuilt, and survived until 31 January 1950. (LTHT)

69 (JF 5005)

Above: Like a number of other municipalities in the United Kingdom in the early 1930s, Leicester City Transport dabbled with the products of Crossley Motors. These were really well manufactured, but suffered from reliability and performance problems that were never really solved by the Manchester-based company. Additionally, they were not easy to drive, and all these factors led to the early withdrawal of 69 (JF 5005) in 1939. After being taken out of service, it was converted into a breakdown lorry and it survived as such until 1949, albeit with a Leyland engine. This bus was a Crossley Condor and, with a Crossley VR6 9.12-litre diesel engine, it was the first oil-engine bus in the Leicester fleet. It was fitted with a Crossley H26/24R body and entered service on 6 November 1933. (R. Marshall Collection)

68 (JF 5010)

Opposite: On a rainy day in January 1934, the policeman on point duty might have been wondering 'what's the point!' With only a brand-new bus – 68 (JF 5010) – for company, his is a lonely and wet world as he stops the bus coming out of Haymarket and, by way of the Clock Tower, across the junction into High Street. It is showing Melbourne Road 26, before route numbers were universally adopted in the city. The Clock Tower is one of Leicester's most famous structures, but it was proposed by some eminent Victorian businessmen in order to occupy a space where the old Hay Market had been. It was begun on March 16 1868 and completed in just twelve weeks after work began. It survives as a symbol of civic pride but, in reality, it was actually built as a nineteenth-century road traffic island at a point where five roads meet in the centre of Leicester. (Leyland Motors)

74 (JF 5877)

The faded wartime white paint on the edges of the wings serves as a reminder of the recent hostilities, as the renumbered 274 (JF 5877) stands in St Nicholas Street on 27 November 1945. It is passing the shoe shop owned by J. E. Townsend. The clean lines of the metal-framed bodies built by Metro-Cammell were very modern-looking for their time. The chassis was a Leyland Titan TD3 and had a Leyland 8.6-litre diesel engine. The first deliveries of this new bus chassis were made to Blackpool Corporation in August 1933, and it remained in production only until early 1935. There were twenty-five Leicester TD3s, and the first five were delivered in the winter of 1933. All of the buses, including those numbered 70 to 89, weighed 6 tons, 10.5 cwt and their robust construction enabled some to achieve a fifteen-year service life. (LTHT)

281 (JF 5884)

On a cold-looking 29 December 1943, the crew of the Leyland Titan TD3 sit in the shelter of the lower saloon. 281 (JF 5884) is at the Braunstone Estate terminus of the 37 route. When compared to the previous Titan TD2, the chassis had a more up-to-date radiator and an engine bay that was only 4 feet, 5 inches long; this allowed the lower saloon bulkhead to be moved forward, thereby increasing the seating capacity downstairs to twenty-six, although Leicester stuck with two fewer. The bus is fitted with all the necessary wartime blackout accessories, while the radiator badge reveals that the bus had been fitted with a radiator from one of the later TD4c gearless buses, when the wartime 'make do and mend' philosophy had presumably come into operation. Parked behind the bus is a Wolseley 12/48 Series III police car, dating from 1938, whose officers have got out of their vehicle. (LTHT)

284 (JF 5887)

Above: Turning into Green Lane Road from the dual carriageway in Coleman Road in October 1945 is 284 (JF 5887). This was one of the twenty Leyland Titan TD3s delivered in the summer of 1934 and fitted with a fifty-seat Metro-Cammell body. Just in front of where the bus is turning was the terminus of the Coleman Road tram route, which turned off Uppingham Road before terminating at this junction on a short length of reserved track. This tram route had replaced the original pioneering Tilling-Stevens TS6s on 31 March 1927, but was itself closed on 23 October 1938; an extended bus service was introduced into an area of recently developed housing. On the near left corner of Coleman Road is the Full Moon Hotel, built in the 1930s in a vaguely roadhouse art deco style. (LCT/LTHT)

286 (JF 5889)

Opposite above: 286 (JF 5889), a 1934 Leyland Titan TD3 with MCCW body, was involved in an accident on Swain Street bridge on 29 March 1946. Many of the thirty passengers on board were injured, as was the conductress, who was in the upper saloon at the time collecting fares. At first sight, 286 doesn't look too badly damaged, but close examination of the rear dome just above the open rear upper saloon emergency exit reveals considerable buckling to the roof. As a result, 286 never ran again, and was broken up for spare parts soon afterwards. The driver was deemed responsible for the accident and was dismissed from his employment. The withdrawal of 286 resulted in the ordering of the solitary PD1A 252 (ERY 386), which entered service on 1 May 1947. Attending the accident is former bus 69 (JF 5005), the 1933 Crossley Condor bus converted to a breakdown lorry in September 1939. (LTHT)

1 (ABC 31)

Above: Parked alongside the Church of the Holy Apostles in Imperial Avenue, just short of Sweetbriar Road, on 22 September 1956 is 1 (ABC 31), a few days before it was withdrawn from service. This twenty-year-old Leyland Tiger TS7c had an MCCW B34R body, whose longevity was due to its metal-framed construction. These buses were purchased to replace the twenty-five-seat Guy Bs of 1927 and 1929. It is working on the Outer Circle 89 route. The church was built in 1924, to the designs of architects Pick, Everard & Keay, at the time of the creation of the new parish off Narborough Road. (D. M. Bailey)

2 (ABC 32)

Above: The line-up of buses in Abbey Park Garage in 1936 shows them posed in chronological order, with at least three of the surviving Guy Bs at the far end. Next to them are six of the normal-control six-wheel Guy CXs. The remaining double-deckers are a motley mixture of Leyland Titan TD1s, TD2s, TD3s and TD4cs; what dates the view is the nearest bus, which is one of the then-brand-new Metro-Cammell-bodied Leyland Tiger TS7c single-deckers. The ten buses that comprised this order were numbered 1 to 10, and were delivered to Leicester during July and August 1936. This was some three months after the arrival of the ABC-registered TD4c double-deckers, one of which is the third bus in the line-up. The single-decker is the almost brand-new 2 (ABC 32), which was renumbered in coronation year to 202. It was one of the last two of the class to be withdrawn, leaving service in February 1958. (LCT)

203 (ABC 33)

Opposite above: On All Fool's Day 1950, a 1936 torque-converter gearbox Leyland Tiger TS7c – 203 (ABC 33) – turns left out of Gipsy Lane, which was lined with interwar council houses, as it negotiates some roadworks at the junction with Catherine Street. The Metro-Cammell B34R metal-framed bodied single-decker bus is working on the 39 service to Overton Road from its terminus in Marfitt Street. It is being followed by a Vauxhall Light Six DY saloon and, behind the road roller, an Austin 10/4 saloon. These ten Leicester City Transport Leyland Tiger TS7cs were quite unusual in that they had bodies built in Birmingham by Metro-Cammell, rather than by Weymann at Addlestone, who were part of the Metro-Cammell-Weymann group. There were rare cases that did not fit this rule, such as the seventeen ARA-registered Leyland Tiger TS6cs delivered to Chesterfield in 1934, and these ten similar buses for Leicester, which all had MCCW metal-framed bodywork. (*Leicester Evening Mail*)

207 (ABC 37)

Above: Standing at the entrance to Bread Street Garage in 1952 is 207 (ABC 37), which is about to be used on a factory duty. The Bread Street Garage off Humberstone Gate, adjacent to the Bell Hotel, had initially been a horse tram depot before becoming the electric tram permanent way stores. In 1922 it was converted to take fourteen trams and after 1950 it became a small capacity garage and parking area behind the Corporation's Transport Department's city-centre offices. It was closed in 1969 to make way for the development of the Haymarket Shopping Centre and was replaced by new premises on Rutland Street. (D. Williams)

209 (ABC 173)

Above: Working on the 39 route is a rather dirty-looking MCCW B34R-bodied Leyland Tiger TS7c. 209 (ABC 173) entered service in August 1936, and was withdrawn after part of the roof of Abbey Park Road Garage collapsed in a gale on 7 November 1952, destroying the body of 209. One of the specific routes for which these single-deckers were intended was the Abbey Lane, Marfitt Street and Overton Road service, which terminated just off Uppingham Road. 209 turns off Overton Road into Quenby Street on 23 March 1952 as it travels to its nearby terminus behind the Sovereign Cinema, well laden with passengers. These buses had their torque-converter gearboxes removed during 1947, so this bus is still equipped with the header tank on the bulkhead, which lubricated the gearbox with a paraffin-and-oil mixture. (R. Marshall)

91 (ABC 176), 80 (JF 5883)

Opposite above: Parked in Bowling Green Street at the rear of the Town Hall, on 17 May 1948, are two Corporation buses, which at first sight look identical. The nearest bus is 91 (ABC 176), a Leyland Titan TD4c with a Metro-Cammell H26/26R body, dating from May 1936. By now, it has been renumbered 291 and fitted with a conventional gearbox. To the rear is 80 (JF 5883), renumbered to 280. This is a Leyland Titan TD3, which had entered service in June 1934. One way of identifying a Leicester Corporation Metro-Cammell-bodied Leyland TD3 from a TD4c is that the later buses had a running strip, which split the lower panels and made replacing the bottom of one of the lower side panels both easier and cheaper! The Leyland TD4cs had Leyland's 'gearless' torque-converter gearbox, as it was easier to use than a normal manual gearbox, especially for former tramcar drivers. Unfortunately, it was the cause of poor fuel-consumption figures; consequently, in 1947, the Leicester buses had these gearboxes removed in favour of a normal four-speed crash gearbox after experiencing poor traction and skidding in the appalling weather conditions during the winter of 1946–47. (R. Marshall)

93 (ABC 178), 94 (ABC 179), 97 (ABC 182)

Above: Three Metro-Cammell-bodied Leyland Titan TD4cs stand in Humberstone Gate, opposite the subterranean toilets with their elaborate wrought ironwork in the middle of the road. They are outside Lewis's newly opened department store, built in 1936 in the company's rather brutal version of the art deco school of architectural design. This was the same year as these buses entered service. On the right, behind the 1936 Leicestershire-registered American Hudson Six saloon, is bus 93 (ABC 178). It is about to leave the city centre on 3 April 1939 as it works the 30 route to Imperial Avenue, Braunstone. This was the first day that buses began to use this part of Humberstone Gate outside Lewis's department store as a city-centre terminal point. Overtaking it is 94 (ABC 179), working to the centre of the Braunstone Estate on the 21 route. Parked in the distance is 97 (ABC 182), being used on the Glenfield Road 31 route. Both buses 93 and 94 are carrying side-mounted route boards. (*Leicester Evening Mail*)

96 (ABC 181), 315 (BRY 377)

Still wearing its pre-war livery is the renumbered 296 (ABC 181), one of the 1936 Metro-Cammell-bodied Leyland Titan TD4cs. It is standing at the front of a line of Corporation buses, awaiting spectators from the greyhound stadium on 17 July 1948. The buses behind include 315 (BRY 377), one of the nine 1937 AEC Regent 0661s with very distinctive Northern Counties bodies, and the solitary Pickering-bodied unfrozen Leyland Titan TD7 347 (DRY 324), delivered in May 1942. The stadium was located north of the central part of Leicester, off the Blackbird Road; the exact site today would be where Somerset Avenue meets Parker Drive. The track, opened in 1923 and initially staged greyhound racing but, after 1928, was also used for speedway with a dedicated cinder oval inside the grassed greyhound track. After thirty years of slow decline and the lack of investment, the stadium site was sold to Barratt Homes for housing and the last meeting took place on 15 September 1984. (R. Marshall)

1937–1942: The Final Pre-War Bus Fleet

301 (BRY 263)

Travelling past the impressive entrance colonnade of the LMS Railway's London Road station on 1 May 1938 is 301 (BRY 263). The bus, a Leyland Titan TD5c with a Leyland H27/26R body, entered service in November 1937; it had the briefly fashionable lack of front headlights, with one nearside driving light in the normal fog-light position. Some municipalities favoured this arrangement on the grounds that on well-illuminated urban roads these low-mounted lights cut through smoggy conditions more effectively. Needless to say, new PSV regulations made this practice illegal on the grounds of safety. 301 is still equipped with side-mounted wooden destination slip boards as it works on the 31 service to Evington via Evington Lane. On 7 May 1947, 301 completely lost its roof and upper deck when the driver inadvertently drove the bus under the low railway bridge in nearby Lancaster Road. Despite only having another three years of service with Leicester, it was reconstructed with a brand new Leyland top deck, similar to those fitted to the PD1s. (H. N. James)

303 (BRY 265)

Above: Turning through Northampton Square in March 1944 is 303 (BRY 265). This is a Leyland H27/26R-bodied Leyland Titan TD5c, which entered service in November 1937. It is being used on the 31 service to Evington, and is travelling towards London Road. Behind the bus is the austere headquarters of the Leicester City police force in Charles Street. This building was designed in 1933 by G. Noel Hill in an English palazzo-cum-art deco style. It has three faces, the smaller five-bay section on the right in St George Street, a corniced central section with a carriage entrance, and wrought iron gates and the longer seven-bay section fronting Charles Street. Charles Street was an up-to-the-minute dual carriageway, created to relieve the pressure of the increasing city-centre traffic in 1931, although it never achieved the status of an important central shopping street. (LTHT)

309 (BRY 271)

Opposite above: Gearless Leyland-bodied Leyland Titan TD5c, which had entered service in November 1937, stands in Humberstone Gate on 17 July 1948 while awaiting passengers when working on the 26 service. These buses were the first in the fleet to have the Colin Bailey-designed five-bay construction body, which had been introduced in July 1937. Torque-converter Titans tended to be quite heavy, and the Leicester ones weighed in at 6 tons, 18 cwt. This resulted in the seating capacity being lowered to a H27/26R layout, in order to conform to the then-current tilt-test PSV regulations. The torque-converter gearboxes were removed in 1947, although 309 appears still to be equipped with this type of gearing, as it has retained the header tank for the gearbox oil on the bulkhead below the front lower saloon window. (R. Marshall)

310 (BRY 272)

Above: Loading up with a full complement of passengers is Leyland-bodied Leyland Titan TD5c 310 (BRY 272). It is about to leave the city centre on the 26 service to Knighton Lane via Welford Road. Whereas many other operators managed to squeeze around sixteen or more years out of similar Leyland-bodied Leylands, Leicester withdrew all theirs in 1950 when they were only thirteen years old. They apparently had plenty of life left in them, as many of these Leylands went on to have extended lives after their sale. Of the twelve buses in the batch, five were exported to the South Western Omnibus Company in Colombo, Ceylon in April 1951, including 310. The bus is standing in Horsefair Street at the side of Leicester Town Hall on 28 May 1949. The imposing Queen Anne-styled town hall was constructed between 1874 and 1876 and was designed by Francis Hames. (R. Marshall)

313 (BRY 375)

A somewhat speculative purchase was made in the late summer of 1937, when nine Northern Counties-bodied AEC Regent 0661s were purchased. These buses, numbered 312 to 320 by Leicester City Transport, had originally been ordered as part of a batch of fifteen vehicles by Cardiff Corporation, intended to be registered in the ABO series. Unfortunately, due to the order becoming surplus to requirements due to Cardiff Corporation's financial difficulties, nine of the order, which were near completion with chassis numbers in the 06615150–64 batch, were offered by AEC for immediate sale. Cardiff retained only fleet numbers 167 to 172 (ABO 970–975), and the remaining nine were diverted to Leicester, entering service during September and October 1937. Cardiff retained the original ABO-registration marks and, within months, another nine identical AEC Regent 0661s had arrived in the Welsh capital, but with later chassis numbers in the sequence 066154178–25. They were the first batch of AEC Regents to be purchased and, along with having an AEC 7.57-litre engine, they also had the advantage of a preselector gearbox. Despite this, these buses were not very popular with drivers. A rather tired-looking 313 (BRY 375) is working on the 14 New Parks Estate service, just south of Groby Road near to Glenfield Hospital during 1950, and stands in the city centre at the Belgrave Gate end of Charles Street. (D. R. Harvey Collection)

318 (BRY 380)

Still wearing its original livery is 318 (BRY 380). This was one of the 1937 AEC Regents originally intended for Cardiff Corporation, but diverted to Leicester. The fifteen buses that were originally ordered by Cardiff, apparently to the specification of their general manager, Mr W. Forbes. They had five-bay metal-framed Northern Counties bodywork, dominated by a rounded styling that took curvature to a new excess. An extremely thick pillared front dome, coupled to an almost mirror-image rear dome, an exaggeratedly bulbous cab apron, out-swept lower saloon panels and D-shaped lower saloon windows completed the body's design. These buses were among the first to be constructed by the Wigan-based coachbuilder to this curvaceous, almost-art deco body design. The buses were painted in Cardiff Corporation's layout, but in Leicester's maroon; this had the cream paintwork around the upper saloon body pillars, which merged into a deep-cream band below the windows and above the large destination screen. The bus standing in Charles Street in front of the premises of J. W. Hemmings, with Yeoman Lane to its rear, as it works on the 27 route to Coleman Road in 1944. (D. R. Harvey Collection)

319 (BRY 381)

Above: Waiting for passengers in Horsefair Street alongside the town hall, with Barclays Bank in the distance on the far side of Every Street, when barely one year old is 319 (BRY 381). This AEC Regent o661 was fitted with a Northern Counties H30/26R body and had entered service in October 1937. It is in as-new condition. These metal-framed buses weighed 6 tons, 13 cwt, three-quarters unladen, which was some four hundredweight lighter than the previous batch of Leyland-bodied Leyland Titan TD5cs. The bus is working on the 26 route to Knighton Lane, and is equipped with wooden side slip destination boards in order to assist any potential passengers. Parked opposite the bus, outside Baxter's Leather Company, is a Vauxhall Light Six four-door saloon, dating from 1936. (LTHT)

321 (CBC 913)

Opposite above: Parked behind the Town Hall in Bowling Green Street is 321 (CBC 913), numerically the first of the AEC Renown o664s. The first nine of these six-wheelers was bodied by Northern Counties, and had a H32/32R seating layout. Weighing 8.25 tons, these buses were a late flowering of the six-wheel double-decker concept, which, by 1939, was only being employed on large-capacity trolleybus chassis. Some of the members of the Transport Committee were enthusiastically lobbying for the introduction of trolleybuses on certain tram routes, but this was met with stern resistance by Mr Ben England, Leicester's highly respected general manager. The purchase of the large-capacity six-wheeler AEC Renown chassis was seen as something of a compromise, as it had three axles and a large seating capacity as per a trolley bus; it was economical but not a trolleybus! 321 is soon to be working on the 24 service to Wigston Lane after its crew have taken their break between journeys. To the rear of the bus is a Morris Eight Series E two-door saloon. (D. Williams)

323 (CBC 915)

Above: The first AEC Renown 0664 to be delivered to Leicester was 323 (CBC 915), which arrived in Leicester in late February 1939, but probably entered service with all the others of the class on 3 April 1939. It is working on the 37 service, and is standing in Narborough Road on 12 March 1944, fully equipped for operation at night during the blackout. The 0664s had a wheelbase of 18 feet and 7 inches. The first batch of the Renowns was bodied by Northern Counties, and had the same features as the previous nine two-axle AEC Regent 0661s; however, because of their extra length, they had six-bay construction bodies. The Northern Counties-bodied examples could be identified when compared to the Metro-Cammell examples of the following year, as they had a more bulbous cab apron below the windscreen, slightly less rounded D-shaped lower saloon windows and shorter side windows in the front domes. The buses weighed 8 tons, 4.5 cwt and carried sixty-four passengers; however, with only an AEC 7.57-litre engine and a preselector gearbox, they were not exactly nimble and struggled to achieve 30 mph, albeit in comfort and a certain degree of style. Their stately progress resulted in them being known as 'Queen Mary's'. (W. J. Haynes)

328 (CBC 920)
Above: Parked alongside a Midland Red SOS FEDD in about 1956 is 328 (CBC 920). The bus is standing in St Margaret's bus station when working on a Gilroes duty. This Northern Counties-bodied AEC Renown 0664 is still in the original livery style, with cream windows in each saloon, although the upper saloon front-window pillars have been painted crimson. A further economy was made by the removal and plating over of the small, rectangular side destination box over the rear nearside D-shaped window. These 1939 deliveries were the first Renowns built by AEC for the home market for well over a year, but there might have been more for Leicester, had production of the model not been stopped after the delivery of the 1940 DBC-registered six-wheelers. (P. J. Marshall)

329 (CBC 921)
Opposite above: The last of the Northern Counties-bodied AEC Renown 0664s to be withdrawn was 329 (CBC 921). This occurred in May 1958 and, within two months, it was sold to the Vintage Passenger Vehicle Society for preservation. This was one of the first 'provincial' buses to be purchased for preservation in the UK, and it remained with the organisation until 1973, when it passed to Leicester Corporation Museum department in March 1973. Extensively restored during the 1980s, 329 is being used on a tour of Leicester on 4 June 1994. It is standing opposite New Romney Crescent in Nether Hall Road, in company with the author's preserved 2489 (JOJ 489), the former Birmingham City Transport 1950 Crossley-bodied Crossley DD42/6. A noteworthy feature of the Leicester bus is the lack of headlights, which gives the frontal appearance of the bus a somewhat-naked appearance. (D. R. Harvey)

332 (DBC 223)

Above: With the imposing walls of HMP Leicester looming tall in the distance, 332 (DBC 223) is in Welford Road near to Leicester Tigers' rugby ground when working on the 26 service in November 1956. All twenty-five of Leicester's Renowns were notable for having the A173 direct-injection 7.57 engines, a D132 pre-selective gearbox, fully floating rear axles and the later pattern of long radiator. With sixty-four-seat double-deck bodies by Metro-Cammell, they had a seating capacity that was slightly more than Leicester's later tramcars. The traces of the tram tracks in the road had been those to Welford Road, but this route had been abandoned on 13 March 1949. This tram route to Clarendon Park via Welford Road was the first new tramway to be built in Leicester after the initial burst of constructing the first twelve routes, culminating with the Melton Road service that had opened in June 1905. This commenced on 26 September 1922, some eighteen years after the previous new route. The route was somewhat 'over run' by the 26 bus service along Welford Road towards the newly developed outer suburbs. (B. Coney)

341 (DBC 232)

Above: Standing majestically on the forecourt of Abbey Park Road Garage on 21 December 1943 is 337 (DBC 228). This Metro-Cammell-bodied AEC Renown 0664 entered service in June 1940 and was among the final Renowns to be built and is in the condition that it was delivered. The uniquely styled metal-framed MCCW bodies were a good copy of the earlier NCME-bodied Renowns of 1939, but proved to be more robust. At the front, the cab apron was less bulbous; the D-shaped windows in the lower saloon had a different profile. The rear dome had a squarer appearance while the less curved front dome arrangement gave the bus a more purposeful appearance. Despite the privations of the wartime conditions, 341 still retains its chromed wheel nut guard rings on all three axles. Despite their large carrying capacity, the Renowns were underpowered and slow with a top speed of barely 30 mph. The rear bogie was similar to the AEC 664T trolleybus, which was expensive to maintain and resulted in heavy tyre wear due to 'scrubbing'. (LTHT)

344 (DBC 235)

Above: The penultimate Metro-Cammell-bodied AEC Renown o664 was 344 (DBC 235); had it not been for the Second World War, Leicester City Transport would have returned to Southall for further examples of these high-capacity six-wheelers. By 1939, the Corporation was contemplating the gradual withdrawal of their tram routes, which was to be postponed by the outbreak of hostilities, and the sixty-four-seater capacity of the Renowns was comparable with those of the fleet of four-wheel trams. 344 travels along Belvoir Street and passes Market Street as it leaves the city centre on its way to Wigston Lane on the 23 route in 1955. The tall Victorian building behind the bus was occupied by Joseph Johnson, who was a ladies and gentleman's outfitter, tailor and draper who had within the store a ladies' hairdressers and a restaurant. (D. Williams)

337 (DBC 228)

Opposite above: Metro-Cammell-bodied AEC Renown 337 (DBC 228) is in Southfields Drive in the south of the city, during August 1955, as it works on the 25 service. 335 is one of the sixteen AEC Renown o664 six-wheelers, with MCCW H32/32R bodywork dating from May 1940. The area was typical of the 1930s municipal housing estates built in the outer suburbs of Leicester after the decision had been made to consolidate rather than extend the existing tramway system. Thus Saffron Lane, displayed on the destination blind of the bus, was never a tram route. 337 is carrying an advertisement for Ediswan, who was an English manufacturer of incandescent lamp bulbs and other electrical goods. It was formed in 1883 by the amalgamation of the British section of the American Edison Company and the Swan Electric Light Company Limited. The Metro-Cammell-bodied Renowns were slightly lighter than the earlier ones with Northern Counties bodies, and had an unladen weight of 8 tons 3.75 cwt. This, combined with their small AEC 7.57-litre oil engines, meant that the Renowns were underpowered and slow, with a top speed of barely 30 mph. The rear bogie was similar to the AEC 664T trolleybus, which was expensive to maintain and resulted in heavy tyre wear due to 'scrubbing'. (D. F. Parker)

346 (DRY 323)

Unloading at the Braunstone Lane terminus of the 22 route on 19 February 1949 is Leicester's first 'unfrozen' double-decker. 346 (DRY 323) was the first of just six Leyland Titan TD7s buses to have MoWT-styled Brush highbridge bodywork; the other five being a pair each for Barrow Corporation and East Yorkshire Road Car, and a solitary example for the independent operator Hants & Sussex. The body was a very severe interpretation of the government regulations, with shallow panels between the wheelbase and square upper saloon front-dome side windows, and the typical 'lobster'-shaped rear dome, which was produced to eliminate any panel-beating, being constructed of angled flat pieces of sheet metal. Nonetheless, the attractive Leicester livery hid many of the 'utility' features of the Brush bodywork. It lasted in service until June 1957. (R. Marshall)

347 (DRY 324)

A long queue of spectators is attempting to get on 347 (DRY 324), which stands at the front of a line of Corporation buses about to leave the Greyhound stadium on 17 July 1948. Unusually, the Corporation managed to avoid being allocated any wartime Daimlers or Guys. 347 arrived in May 1942, with an uncompromising-looking body built by Pickering of Wishaw. Strangely, the bodies of all the wartime Pickering products had chrome-finished windscreen and opening window trims, which looked somewhat incongruous on a vehicle body lacking any apparent nod towards luxury. Of the eight TD7s fitted with Pickering bodies, only two went to English operators, with one going to Northampton Corporation as their 111 (VV 8747), and the other being a Leicester Corporation bus. Unfortunately, the unseasoned timber used by Pickering seemed to be more unseasoned than most and, very quickly, the poor reputation of these bodies resulted in early withdrawals. After withdrawal on 1 November 1950, 347 was cut down to a single decker due to the poor state of the upper deck and, for seven months from 1 April 1950, ran as a B26R single-decker before being taken out of service and stored until it was eventually officially withdrawn on 9 February 1955. (R. Marshall Collection)

1946–1948: Early Post-War, Pre-Tram-Abandonment Buses

211 (DJF 324)

The bodies on the nine Park Royal-bodied AEC Regent II 0661s were built to the relaxed utility specification, and all of them entered service in February and March 1946. They were numbered 211 to 219 and had chassis numbers interspersed with Leicester's Weymann-bodied Regent IIs. Because of a chronic shortage of single-deck vehicles, Leicester's 211 to 215 and 217 were exchanged in July 1952 for six of Devon General's AEC Regal II 0662s, with Weymann B35F bodies that also dated from 1946. The Regals became Leicester's 195 to 200, while the Leicester Regents became Devon General's DR101 to 106. 211 (DJF 324), in the full red-and-white livery of Devon General, is parked after having worked the 51 service in about 1953; it still retains the Leicester destination and route number boxes. (D. R. Harvey Collection)

218 (DJF 331)

The stark utility shape of the Park Royal bodywork didn't really do the post-war AEC Regent II 0661/20 any favours, as it looked just like a wartime double-decker. The Regent II was basically the reintroduced pre-war model, and was characterised by having a radiator that was mounted quite high over the AEC 7.57-litre diesel engine, which was coupled to a crash gearbox. The Park Royal body was of the 'relaxed' utility style. This had extra opening windows in each saloon and a slightly shaped rear dome, though it was still a rather stark-looking vehicle. 218 (DJF 331) stands at the 29 route terminus at Stoneygate in December 1958. The bus entered service with Leicester in 1946, and the late 1950s advertisement for 'Crawford Cream Crackers'. 218 was withdrawn in June 1959 and sold to North's at Sherburn-in-Elmet, who quickly broke it up. (D. R. Harvey Collection)

219 (DJF 332)

Above: Standing in Charles Street in May 1947 is 219 (DJF 332). The bus is carrying an advertisement for Puro Soap Powder, who were a Leeds-based firm. This Park Royal-bodied AEC Regent II 0661 was barely one year old, having entered service in March 1946. The wartime origins of the bodywork are obvious and, although the Park Royal bodies had a 'utility' outline, they were built to what was termed a 'relaxed' style and weighed only 6 tons, 18 cwt. With their slightly better interior finish, they were better to ride on than genuine wartime buses, such as Guy Arab IIs, which Leicester somehow managed to avoid being allocated. Still, the Park Royal-bodied AEC Regent II looked 'utility' and was a barely modified pre-war chassis with a crash gearbox. (W. J. Haynes)

221 (DJF 315)

Opposite above: Picking up passengers outside the drapery shop of W. A. Lea & Sons in Charles Street is 221 (DJF 315). This was the second of nine AEC Regent II 0661s, fitted with the new post-war body built by Weymann of Addlestone. The body design was little different to the last pre-war offerings built by Weymann in 1940, but at least they looked more attractive than their somewhat spartan-looking Park Royal contemporaries. 221 arrived in December 1945 and was licensed for service on 1 January 1946. The high-mounted radiator, small windscreen and sculpted front wings did look a little old-fashioned, although swept skirt panels added a certain distinguished appearance to the Weymann bodywork. 221 is working on the 57 route in November 1957. Parked behind it is Leyland-bodied Leyland Titan PD2/1 112 (FJF 151). (B. Coney)

224 (DJF 319)

Above: Leicester City Transport decorated a number of buses for HM Queen Elizabeth II's coronation. Weymann-bodied AEC Regent II 0661 224 (DJF 319) is parked in Bread Street Garage forecourt on 2 June 1953. Although nowhere near as elaborately decorated as the buses celebrating HM King George V's silver jubilee in May 1935, 224 (DJF 319) entered service in February 1946. However, in common with most of these buses, it was sold two months after its withdrawal on 30 June 1959 to North, the Leeds dealer, whereupon it was broken up. It was the only one of these buses to have a recessed windscreen. In common with a number of other Leicester buses, 224 has its front decorated in coronation-style red, white and blue crepe. Leaving the bus garage and turning into Charles Street is all-Leyland PD2/1 139 (FJF 178). In the background in Charles Street is the mid-1930s Hannam Court shops and flats. (LTHT)

228 (DJF 323)

Above: The AEC Regent II 0661 was a model that was basically the pre-war Regent and was an interim model in production for five years from 1945. The nine Leicester ones, numbered 220 to 228, had Weymann's standard post-war double-deck, metal-framed, five-bay, highbridge bodies; these were 7 feet, 6 inches wide, had a fifty-six-seat rear-entrance open-platform layout and weighed around 7 tons, 3 cwt. Immediately after the war, municipal and BET customers were taking either the AEC Regent II 0661 chassis or the Leyland Titan PD1 vehicles in large quantities. The MoS initial sanction on the AEC Regent II was for eighty such chassis, of which sixty were earmarked to be bodied by Weymann and the rest by Park Royal. Leicester were intended to have three more Regent IIs, to be numbered 229 to 231, but the order was never fulfilled and the fleet numbers never used. 228 (DJF 323) is working on the 18 service to Braunstone Estate in Newarke Street during April 1953. At the barrier behind is a Metro-Cammell-bodied AEC Renown, working on the 22 service to Braunstone Lane. (M. Rooum)

234 (DJF 335)

Opposite: Speeding down London Road in 1955 is 234 (DJF 335), one of the twenty Leyland-bodied Leyland Titan PD1s; it is working on the 38 Humberstone service. The previously chromed radiator grill has been painted red, which rather detracts from its appearance. This bus had entered service with Leicester in June 1946, and would be sold at the end of 1959 to Barton of Chilwell, becoming their 830 and lasting until 1967. 234 is carrying an advertisement for Shipstone's Ales, who were a brewery based in New Basford in Nottingham. Shipstone's opened in 1852 and closed in 1991; although its beers are being advertised on the side of a Leicester City Transport bus, ironically the brewery sponsored nearby Nottingham Forest at the time of their greatest successes under the management of Brian Clough! (D. Williams)

238 (DJF 339)

Above: About to depart from the Melton Road terminus of the 42 route on 3 September 1949
is one of the twenty-one Leyland Titan PD1 with Leyland H30/26R body. The comparison with
101 (FJF 140), a three-years-younger Leyland-bodied Leyland Titan PD2/1, shows how the two
models, if fitted with Leyland bodies, could be identified. The PD1 238, (DJF 339), weighing
just 7 tons, 2 cwt, has the front panel below the windscreen extended over the offside front
wing, whereas the PD2/1's equivalent panel is a lot tidier as it is only extended halfway down
the front wing. The rest of the early post-war Leyland bodywork was similar to that found on
the final pre-war examples, with a rather severe-looking guttering over the upper saloon front
windows; this was omitted on the PD2 Leyland bodywork, giving a 'softer' appearance. The
42 bus turning circle was further out from the city than the original tram terminus. This bus
service had replaced the original tram route, opened on 8 June 1905 and finally abandoned on
3 July 1949. DJF 339 is showing the destination '32 East Park Road via Humberstone Road',
which was coupled with the 42 route for operational purposes. (R. Marshall)

240 (DJF 341)

Opposite above: Working on the route to Melbourne Road is the freshly repainted 240 (DJF
341). It stands near to the passenger stone-arched entrance to London Road railway station
in July 1950. The bus driver is looking in his interior cab mirror in order to anticipate the
conductor pressing the platform bell. 240 is a Leyland Titan PD1 with a Leyland H30/26R
body, which had entered service in October 1946. It had another ten years of service in Leicester
before it was sold to Barton Transport as their 876. The bus is carrying an advertisement for
Crosse & Blackwell, a company that was originally formed in 1704 and, as well as making
soups, also produced relishes, canned fruit and vegetables, baked beans, jams, jellies and the
famous Branston pickle. (S .N. J. White)

242 (DJF 343)

Above: A well-laden 242 (DJF 343), a Leyland Titan PD1 with Leyland H30/26R body, travels westwards towards the city centre as it works the 61 service on 29 December 1962, just one month before it was withdrawn. In 1945, Leyland Motors announced their new Titan PD1, which had the newly designed E181 7.4-litre engine and a good fuel economy, but was not as sophisticated as the pre-war TD7. The gearbox was a four-speed constant-mesh unit, and the model had triple-servo vacuum brakes. A new, larger, radiator was fitted and its filler-cap was offset to the nearside, which enabled the windscreen to be wider than on pre-war Leylands. 242 has just passed beneath the railway bridge in Uppingham Road, with the Humberstone station buildings built as a high-level site just encroaching onto the bridge. The station opened in 1882 as part of the Great Northern Railway and London & North Western Railway joint line from Market Harborough. The line finally closed to regular traffic in 1962. (C. Aston)

252 (ERY 386)

The solitary Leyland Titan PD1A 252 (ERY 386) was a model fitted with Metalastik rubber-bushed spring shackle pins on the suspension. This improved the ride of the bus but, to the average passenger, it looked the same externally as the standard Leyland-bodied PD1s. The bus is working a service extra on the 57 route to Mowmacre Hill. 252 is outside W. A. Lea & Sons in Charles Street on 18 April 1959, some ten months before it was withdrawn. 252 was delivered in May 1947 as an extra bus to replace the pre-war 286 (JF 5889), which was scrapped after turning over in Swain Street on 29 March 1946. (R. Marshall Collection)

1949–1950: The First Tram Replacement Buses

1 (FBC 267)
Working on the 41 route is the first of the Metro-Cammell-bodied AEC Regent III 9612Es. 1 (FBC 267) entered service in July 1949, and the body delivered to Leicester was the standard Metro-Cammell style that had already been delivered to Dundee, Glasgow, Nottingham, Salford and Coventry, having its origins in bodies built at Washwood Heath in the late 1930s. The fleet number series restarted at 1, and this bus was the first of 160 new buses delivered between November 1948 and December 1950 to replace the last of the trams and most of the pre-war buses. On 19 July 1963, 1 is already nearly full up and is about to leave Humberstone Gate. (Photofives)

6 (FBC 272)

Above: 6 (FBC 272) a 1949 AEC Regent 9612E, with a Metro-Cammell H30/26R body, speeds along Humberstone Gate, having left behind the Plough Inn, and is about to pass the offices of the Transport Department. Although the Metro-Cammell-bodied Regent IIIs were numbered 1 to 31, the deliveries of these buses from the bodybuilders was very slow; so much so that, by the time FBC 272 had been delivered, the entire batch of thirty-four Brush-bodied Regents, numbered 32 to 65, had been in service between two and seven months. The bustling city-centre street is full of shoppers and people queuing for their bus home as the driver starts his journey on the 66 route to Melbourne Road, by way of Humberstone Road. (D. R. Harvey Collection)

25 (FBC 291)

Above: Parked on Burleys Lane is 25 (FBC 291), which is about to work on the Inner Circle service more usually operated by a single-decker bus. It appears that the passengers have been brainwashed into thinking that their bus is a single-decker, as the lower saloon is virtually full while the top deck is virtually empty. The AEC Regent 9612E had a fifty-six-seater Metro-Cammell body of a style that could be traced back to the mid-1930s, and was the bodybuilder's standard type on the AEC Regent III chassis. The bus is still quite new, as the front destination boxes remain in their 'as delivered state', with the route number on the nearside of the front panel. Behind the bus is the St Margaret's factory of Nathaniel Corah, who were manufacturers of hosiery, textiles and knitwear. For over fifty years, they were one of the main suppliers of clothing to Marks & Spencer and, for a time, were the largest knitwear producer in Europe. Bus 25 was sold to Hull Corporation in June 1966 as their fleet number 208 and survived until January 1969. (A. D. Packer)

11 (FBC 277)

Opposite below: Parked outside the mock-Tudor AA-recommended White Hart Hotel in Haymarket is a Metro-Cammell-bodied AEC Regent 9612E. 11 (FBC 277) is operating on the 57 route to Mowmacre Hill on 9 May 1958, with flags and bunting decorating most of the buildings in Haymarket for a visit to Leicester by HM the Queen. The White Hart Hotel was demolished in 1976. Behind the bus is the even more impressive half-timbered George Hotel, which also was swept away at the same time. This was where the first horse-bus service in Leicester began on 22 June 1863 from the George Hotel in Haymarket to The White Horse in Oadby. (A. Richardson)

30 (FBC 296)

Above: Travelling along Uppingham Road on 4 June 1961 when working on the 14 route is AEC Regent III 30 (FBC 296). The late delivery of these Metro-Cammell bodies was disappointing, with FBC 296 not arriving in the city until 12 August 1949, some two months after the first buses in the 1 to 31 batch had arrived, and nine months after the first of the Brush-bodied Regent IIIs had been delivered. 30 was first licensed on 1 October 1949. It has just passed beneath Uppingham Road railway bridge at Humberstone station. This railway line from Market Harborough was closed to regular traffic in coronation year, although it remained open for summer weekend specials until 1962. (R. F. Mack)

33 (FBC 299)

Above: In March 1960, working a 24 service journey to Saffron Lane, is 33 (FBC 299). This AEC Regent III 9612E was fitted with a Birmingham-style metal-framed Brush H30/26R body and had entered service on 15 November 1948, being the first of the batch to go on the road. In the spring of 1957, all the Brush-bodied AEC Regents were re-seated to a H33/27R layout. Bus 33 is climbing the hill as it travels southwards, having just passed Duffield Street on the right. The road is lined with a mixture of late-Victorian terraces and larger terraced three-storied housing built at the time of great expansion of the textile industry in the town. (C. Aston)

32 (FBC 298)

Opposite below: The first of the thirty-four Brush-bodied AEC Regent III 9612Es stands at the Loughborough Coachbuilders factory in November 1948, alongside a Birmingham City Transport Leyland Titan PD2/1s, immediately before being delivered to Leicester. The 9612E model had a 9.6-litre engine, a preselector epicyclic gearbox, and air brakes, which made its performance and ease of driving a far better proposition than many of the earlier post-war buses bought by Leicester City Transport. The Leicester buses had angled staircases, thus eliminating their intrusion into the lower saloon and the need for the triangular offside rear window. The Brush bodies built for Leicester were not as robust as the contemporary Birmingham ones, due, in part, to the lower specification for the interior fixtures. They weighed only 7 tons 15 cwt 3 qtrs compared to the BCT PD2/1s, which weighed 6 cwt more, but Leicester still managed to get seventeen years' usage out of them. (Brush)

38 (FBC 304)

Above: 38 (FBC 304) stands in the turning circle in Narborough Road on 19 February 1949; pre-war bus 276 (JF 5879), a Leyland Titan TD3 with a Metro-Cammell H26/24R body dating from 1934, brings up the rear. Both buses are working on the Narborough Road 21 service, but this is definitely the case of 'the King is dead, long live the King', as the AEC is less than a year old and the TD3 is entering its last year in service. The style of the Brush bodywork for Leicester was based on that designed to Birmingham City Transport specifications, and was chosen because of the promise of a fairly quick delivery. There were 101 metal-framed bodies built for BCT with straight staircases (one re-bodied 1939 Daimler COG5 chassis and 100 Leyland Titan PD2/1 chassis). Of the rest, all were built on AEC Regent III chassis with 'normal' staircases; thirty-four went to Leicester, five to the Ebor Bus Company of Mansfield and one to Naylor of Normanton. (R. Marshall)

47 (FBC 313)

Opposite below: 47 (FBC 313) is about to pull away from a bus stop in Evington Lane at Roundhill Road, near the original terminus, when working on the 31 route via London Road in 1959. This was a Brush-bodied AEC Regent III 9612E, which had entered service in December 1948. It was still substantially the same as when it was first delivered, except for the fitting of flashing side direction indicators, which replaced the original trafficator arms, and the swapping of the front destination boxes so that the route-number display is now on the offside of the front panel. These buses were about as long-lived in Leicester as their Metro-Cammell counterparts, but generally survived for more years in service after disposal. (P. Smith)

44 (FBC 310)

Above: Of the thirty-four Brush-bodied AEC Regent III 9612Es, numbered between 32 and 65, twenty-five of them were sold to Wessex Coaches of Bristol between February 1964 and September 1965. They were all painted in an all-over blue livery, given Taylor Woodrow fleet-name stickers and sent to the island of Anglesey. This was to provide staff transport while the Wilfa power station was being constructed just west of Cemaes Bay, located on the coast in order to provide a cooling source for its operation. Wilfa housed two 490 MW Magnox nuclear reactors, built between 1963 and 1971. Former Leicester 44 (FBC 310) is parked at Wilfa along with at least six others of the batch, including the distant 42 (FBC 308). Former 44 survived until January 1969, while 42 was the first to be taken out of service in October 1967. At least eight of the Brush-bodied AEC Regent IIIs lasted until the construction of the nuclear power station was completed in 1971. (R. F. Mack)

63 (FBC 329)

Almost at the Clock Tower in Gallowtree Gate on Wednesday 9 May 1958 is 63 (FBC 329), which is working on the Melton Road 42 service. This Brush-bodied AEC Regent III was one of the extra three that were tacked on to the original order for thirty-one buses to replace the three Weymann-bodied Regent IIs, which were not delivered in 1946. Many of the buildings are decorated with flags and bunting to celebrate the visit to Leicester of HM Queen Elizabeth II on 9 May 1958. The tall building with the arched first floor is the Midland Chambers, which contained offices for an accountant's, Liverpool Victoria Insurance and Thomas Cook travel agents. Turning into Eastgates on the right is a Ford 5-cwt van, converted into a rudimentary estate car by having windows cut into its side panels. Overtaking FBC 329 is a fabric-bodied Morris Minor, dating from 1929 and registered by Norfolk CC. (A. Richardson)

66 (FBC 541)

When Leicester City Transport ordered thirty Daimler CVD6 chassis, the original order was for ten of them to be bodied by Willowbrook of Loughborough and twenty by Charles Roberts of Horbury, near Wakefield. The order for the bodies was reversed when Roberts could not meet the required delivery date. 66 (FBC 541) stands outside the Roberts factory in July 1949. The attractive metal-framed Roberts H30/26R bodies were of a four-bay construction style and were all too well made, as they were very heavy at 8 tons, 3 cwt, 3qtrs unladen. They were fitted with the 8.6-litre Daimler CD6 engine, and were somewhat underpowered when compared to the contemporary AECs and Leylands. Charles Roberts was a railway carriage and wagon builder who periodically built bus bodies. This four-bay body style had been developed in 1946 and remained in production until 1950. (Charles Roberts)

69 (FBC 544)

Above: Travelling out of the city and up the hill in London Road is 69 (FBC544). It is working on the 29 route in 1957. The bus is one of the ten Daimler CVD6s with Roberts H30/26R bodywork, and is being followed by AEC Regent III 9612E with MCCW H30/26R bodywork dating from July 1949. London Road was lined with large Victorian three-storey houses and was always regarded as one of the better residential areas of Leicester, despite its proximity to the city centre. These Daimlers had that company's own CD6 8.6-litre engine, which was very quiet and well suited to passengers wanting a pleasant, quiet ride in a bus. Unfortunately, the CD6 unit was expensive to maintain; it tended to burn engine oil and be prone to overheating if not in top mechanical condition. As a result of these mechanical problems, all but two of the Roberts-bodied examples, including 69, were taken out of service during August and September 1961. (D. Williams)

77 (FBC 660)

Above: The body order for the thirty Daimler CVD6s was reversed, meaning that the buses numbered 76 to 95 received Willowbrook bodies that were made locally in Loughborough. The style of the composite construction bodywork delivered to Leicester was the highbridge version of Willowbrook's standard first post-war design. It had elliptical curved end saloon windows, whose shape were echoed by the round-topped front upper saloon windows and a quite noticeably raked front profile. The second of these twenty buses, 77 (FBC 660), is working on an extra 31 service on 2 May 1959. It has come out of Evington Road, whose entrance behind the bus is guarded by the large vaguely arts-and-crafts Bentley House on the left, and the earlier tall brick Gothic Revival building, which was the Corporation's rent tribunal offices. The bus is turning towards the city centre and is facing the impressive entrance gates to Victoria Park. (M. A. Sutcliffe)

74 (FBC 549)

Opposite below: The driver of the bus makes a half-hearted hand signal to indicate that he is turning right out of Gallowtree Gate into Horsefair Street, where it will stop outside the town hall. 74 (FBC 549) is a Roberts-bodied Daimler CVD6, and is working on the 49 route to Wigston Lane via Aylestone Road in September 1961. Parked outside the premises of F. W. Woolworth is a large two-tone coloured Vauxhall Cresta PA saloon; queuing behind the Bedford TK lorry is an Austin A40 Devon, a Jaguar 2.4-litre Mark 1, an almost brand-new Triumph Herald and, at the rear, a quite rare Riley Pathfinder dating from the mid-1950s. In the distance at the far end of Gallowtree Gate above the Pickford's pantechnicon, the Clock Tower pierces the skyline. (R. F. Mack)

87 (FBC 670)

Standing at the Welford Road terminus of the 26 route on 1 July 1959, facing towards the city centre, is 87 (FBC 670). The bus is standing at one of Leicester's many concrete bus shelters, which provided passengers, particularly at the outer termini, with a good deal of protection at exposed places. These Willowbrook-bodied Daimler CVD6s had entered service between November 1948 and March 1949, and weighed 7 tons, 17¾ cwt, which was considerably lighter than the Roberts-bodied examples. 87 would remain in operation with Leicester City Transport until December 1962, which was about the time when most of these Daimler CD6-engined buses would be withdrawn in favour of new 30-foot-long Leyland Titan PD3A/1s. This was because of the generally poor mechanical longevity of the Daimler engine and its poor oil economy. (A. J. Douglas)

95 (FBC 678)

Just like the Brush-bodied Leyland Titan PD2/1s before them, Wessex Coaches of Bristol bought all twenty Willowbrook-bodied Daimler CVD6s. The first six were sold to Wessex Coaches for £175 each, while 82 to 85 were acquired for £125 each. The last ten, including 95, cost just £100 each. The last of the class, 95 (FBC 678), went to Wessex in March 1963, and stayed with them until June 1966. Painted in an all-over blue livery, with Taylor Woodrow sticker fleet names, it is parked on a piece of waste ground in Felixstowe in August 1965. It would be used to transport workers to the Magnox nuclear power station, which was under construction on the Essex coastline at Bradwell. This produced its first electricity in 1962 and, after further expansion, it closed in its present form in 2002. (D. R. Harvey)

1949–1950: The PD2 Era

97 (FJF 136)

Working on the Melton Road 42 service is 97 (FJF 136), the second of the Leyland-bodied Leyland Titan PD2/1. The first ten of these buses entered service in May 1949; the next ten buses arrived in February 1950, which took the fleet numbers up to 115, while the next ten only arrived in Leicester in the following July. It took until the December before all of the sixty-four PD2/1s were delivered. In May 1958, many of the buildings in Gallowtree Gate are decorated with Union flags for the visit of HM the Queen. The bus has just pulled away from the bus stop, and is approaching the Clock Tower in East Gates and passing Bellman's wool shop. In the distance, parked outside Timpson's shoe shop, is 80 (FBC 663), one of the twenty Daimler CVD6s bodied by Willowbrook and delivered in November 1948. (A. Richardson)

102 (FJF 141)

Double-deckers working on the Inner Circle 48 route were fairly unusual, but it did happen, especially when the one of the fairly small number of single-deckers was unavailable. Leyland Titan PD2/1, with a Leyland H30/26R body, entered service on 1 May 1949. It is parked in Burleys Way, alongside St Margaret's bus station, after it had been re-seated in December 1962 to a H33/29R layout. It is also painted in the post-May-1961 livery of cream with three maroon bands. This was intended to brighten up the bus fleet, and thereby give the buses a more modern look. While it suited the new 30-foot-long buses, on the older PD2/1s the new livery somehow managed to lose the appearance of a dignified municipal pride. (D. R. Harvey Collection)

115 (FJF 154)

Above: Don't take a short cut! Leyland-bodied Leyland Titan PD2/1 115 (FJF 154) was returning from a football-special duty on Saturday 22 February 1958, when the driver decided to take a shortcut underneath the 12-foot, 6-inch-high Lancaster Road railway bridge. The bridge won the contest, as the bus was decapitated, with the whole of the top deck being peeled back and left in the roadway behind the bus. This rather took the shine off Leicester City FC's 8-4 victory at Filbert Street against Manchester City. Fortunately, the bus wasn't carrying any passengers and 115 eventually received a new top deck, re-entering service in September 1958 and surviving until October 1967. It was sold to a dealer called Hibbins, based at Ramsey near Huntingdon, along with nine other Leyland-bodied Leyland PD2/1s. (*Leicester Evening Mail*)

125 (FJF 164)

Above: In Hinckley Road, with Western Park's trees in the distance and late-1920s housing lining the road, a passenger runs for the bus. It was working on the 40 route on 4 June 1960, when it was linked as a cross-city service from Braunstone Estate on route 18 to the Belgrave 40 or 43 routes. 125 (FJF 164), a Leyland Titan PD2/1 with a Leyland H30/26R body, by now has had its seating capacity increased in 1957 to H33/29R. It is about to pull away as it continues towards the city centre. The bus looks very smart in its original crimson-and-cream paintwork layout, although the Corporation failed to use the beading below the upper saloon windows on the Leyland bodywork as a livery feature until the predominantly cream paintwork of 1961 was adopted. The Hinckley Road tram route had opened on 12 July 1904, and lasted as the 1 route until 21 November 1948, when it was replaced by the 17 bus route. (R. F. Mack)

117 (FJF 156)

Opposite below: A Leyland Titan PD2/1, with a Leyland body, cuts across the arrivals entrance to London Road railway station. 117 (FJF 156) is operating on the 31 service to Evington on 9 October 1964. It has just left the city centre and will shortly climb the hill up London Road towards the entrance to Victoria Park. 117 was one of the ten PD2/1s that entered service in July 1950, lasting until March 1968. It was then sold to Tiger Coaches of Salsburgh, Lanarkshire, who acted as a dealer; they, in turn, sold 117 to Derwent Coaches of Swalwell, near Gateshead, in May 1968 for transporting children on school journeys into the towns of the north-east from rural areas. (P. J. Relf)

128 (FJF 167)

Above: Parked in the bus lay-by at the terminus of the 42 route in Melton Road is 128 (FJF 167). It is operating on the cross-city service to East Park Road via London Road on the 33 route; a second route, numbered 32, reached the same destination by way of Humberstone Road. The bus is about one year old and is a Leyland Titan PD2/1 with a Leyland H30/26R body. 128, still equipped with trafficators, had the second style of Leyland body, which was fitted on the PD2 model that had been introduced in late 1948. It had a sloping lower edge to the nearside of the front canopy, providing space for a heater unit if required; a cast-aluminium radiator shell; and pierced front-wheel nut guard rings. (R. Marshall)

135 (FJF 174)

Opposite above: Waiting in the turning circle in Broad Avenue at the entrance to the general hospital is 135 (FJF 174). It is working on the 54 Stocking Farm route on 14 October 1956, and again still has trafficators. 135 entered service in August 1950 and remained with the Corporation until December 1968. The buses were possibly the most successful and reliable buses ever to operate in Leicester. They managed between seventeen and nearly twenty years in frontline service, during which time the majority of them were repainted in the reverse-cream livery and had their seating capacity increased by six to sixty-two. The individual PD2/1 buses were weighed individually but, on average, weighed about 7 tons, 11 cwt; however, on reseating, their weight went up to 7 tons, 13 cwt, 3 qtrs. (R. Marshall)

146 (FJF 185)

Above: The tramway traction poles are still in place around the Clock Tower when 146 (FJF 185), an almost-new Leyland Titan PD2/1 with a Leyland H30/26R body, waits outside Jax gown shop in Gallowtree Gate. The shoppers are out in force in this central part of the city where all the large department stores were located. However, even by the early 1950s, the lack of spending power meant that many of the people were only window shopping. Behind the bus, Humberstone Gate is to the right of the Gold Flake cigarette advertisement, while in the distance is Haymarket. The bus is working on the 33 service to East Park Road, by way of London Road, in about 1952. (R. Marshall)

149 (FJF 188)

Above: 149 (FJF 188) is travelling along Abbey Street alongside St Margaret's bus station and is about to reach Burleys Way. The bus is a Leyland Titan PD2/1, whose Leyland body by this date sat sixty-two passengers and is in the cream livery. It is being used on a very-well-patronised 72 service to Mowmacre Hill in the north of the city. Behind the bus is the impressive seven-storey Abbey Street car park that, when it was completed in November 1969, was the largest multi-storey car park in Britain. The car parked opposite the bus is a Ford Anglia 100E two-door saloon. (R. H. G. Simpson)

160 (FJF 199)

Above: After receiving sixty-four Leyland Titan PD2/1s, Leicester City Transport received a final Leyland-bodied bus. This was a new model built to the increased Construction and Use Regulations, and was the latest 8-foot wide and 27-inch-long PD2/12 type. The bus was 160 (FJF 199) and the extra foot in length enabled the seating capacity to be raised by four to an H32/28R layout. It is in Humberstone Gate on the morning of 4 August 1969, and has just pulled away from the 38 stop near to the Admiral Nelson public house. Opposite is the large John Lewis department store, which was built in 1936 and occupied a large expanse of Humberstone Gate. 160 was exhibited at the 1950 Earls Court Commercial motor show on the Leyland stand, and was the first of two production PD2/12s to be built with chassis number 502823. The bus had a sixty-seat version of the new style of Leyland body, with curved corners and window pans. Its extra width was identifiable by the inward taper of the front bay of the upper-saloon body, as the front of the Leyland used standard 7-foot, 6-inch front panels, while the rest of the body was 6 inches wider. 160 was an early recipient of the all-over cream livery with three crimson bands that had been introduced in May 1961; this was applied to 160 when it re-entered service on 25 June 1965. (D. J. Little)

154 (FJF 193)

Opposite below: Leaving the Showbus Rally at Duxford on 27 September 2009 is the quite splendidly preserved 154 (FJF 193), the sole surviving Leicester City Transport Leyland-bodied Leyland PD2/1. After withdrawal, 154 was sold to Fisher & Ford, a Barnsley bus dealer and scrap merchant, in April 1970. It was used for a long time by a farmer in West Butterwick in North Lincolnshire, on the western bank of the River Trent, as a non-PSV staff bus for his strawberry pickers. It eventually arrived at Joe Sykes (dealer), Carlton, in September 1981 and was returned to Leicester City Transport in exchange for the withdrawn Leyland PD3A GRY 63D. The Corporation undertook a complete restoration to full PSV standard, which was completed in July 1983. After passing to the First Bus Group, it was sold to a private owner in 2008 and continues to thrive in preservation. (D. R. Harvey)

1950s and 1960s Single-Deckers

195 (HTT 484)

HTT 484 was new in July 1946 to Devon General as their SR 484. This AEC Regal II 0662 had a Weymann B35F body, and was the first of six single-deckers that were acquired by Leicester City Transport in July 1952 for use on the proposed Inner and Outer Circle services. They were exchanged for six of Leicester's 'relaxed utility-style' Park Royal-bodied AEC Regent 0661s, which had been numbered 211 to 215 and 217. Those buses intended for use on the Inner Circle 48 service were fitted with roof route boards. HTT 484 became 195 in the Corporation fleet. They were intended to replace the ten 1936 Leyland Tiger TS7c but, with a smaller engine of 7.57-litre capacity, an increase in weight of 12 cwt and a constant mesh gearbox, the Regal IIs were not popular with drivers. 195 is parked in Charles Street after its conversion to one-man-operation. In this form, the four converted buses could be easily distinguished by the diagonal window over the rear of the engine and the partial removal of the bulkhead behind the driver. (P. Yeomans)

196 (HTT 486)

Parked at the terminus of the 39 route behind the Shaftesbury Cinema in Houghton Street, in about 1954, is 196 (HTT 486). This was one of the six former Devon General AEC Regal II 0662s with Weymann B35F bodywork, new in July 1946. The Regal IIs were repainted by Devon General into Leicester's livery, prior to their arrival in the East Midlands. The 39 route ceased to exist in this form after October 1954, when the replacement route was converted to double-deck operation as part of the new Outer Circle 89 route scheme. 196 was converted to one-man-operation by Leicester City Transport in May 1956, at which time it was also re-seated to B34F. (A. D. Packer)

200 (HTT 504)

Above: 200 (HTT 504) is parked in Burleys Way, just outside St Margaret's bus station, when operating as an o-m-o vehicle on the 48 Inner Circle service, which is prominently displayed on the roof-mounted slip boards. 200 was one of two from the acquired six Weymann-bodied AEC Regal II 0662s that were down-seated to just twenty-eight passengers in March 1954, the other being 195. 200 was later re-seated to a B34F layout and stayed in service until December 1963, before eventually passing to a Fort William contractor. There it survived until at least July 1965 to become the last of the six acquired Regal IIs to remain operational. (R. Marshall)

191 (OJF 191)

Opposite above: 191 (OJF 191) was new to Leicester City Transport in October 1956. It was the first of the batch of four Weymann Hermes-bodied, underfloor-engined Leyland Tiger Cub PSUC1/1 single-deck buses, numbered 191 to 194. They cost £3,926 2s 1d each, with the chassis amounting to £1,888 7s 1d and the body £2,037 15s 0d. They had the route name 'OUTER CIRCLE' painted on the exterior cove panel roof sides. Their seating capacity of forty-four gave them a useful extra ten seats over the 1936 Metro-Cammell metal-framed bodied Leyland Tiger TS7cs that they replaced. The Tiger Cubs, in a change of Corporation policy, had registration numbers that coincided with their fleet numbers. This was useful for identification purposes for drivers and garage staff, as well as bus enthusiasts! 191 is in the Broad Avenue turning circle at the entrance to the General Hospital when working on the 89 route. (R. Marshall)

212 (SJF 212)

Above: 212 (SJF 212) was a Leyland Tiger Cub, designated PSUC1/1T, bought as an extra vehicle and delivered in March 1958. It had a Weymann B44F body and was fitted with a Leyland o.350 5.76-litre horizontal engine, a five-speed constant mesh gearbox and a two-speed axle. The five underfloor-engined buses were also used in their earlier years on private-hire duties. After 1961, they were repainted in the mainly cream livery with crimson skirt panelling, and all five of the single-deckers were converted to one-man operation. It is travelling along Abbey Street alongside St Margaret's bus station on 22 May 1965 when being underused on the 48 Inner Circle service. (R. H. G. Simpson)

196 (ABC 196B)

Above: Leicester City Transport's next foray into the single-deck market began in December 1963, with the delivery of four AEC Reliance 4MU3RA. These had attractive Marshall B54F bodies that had been developed by the Cambridge-based bodybuilder in conjunction with the BET Group. 196 (ABC 196B), bought for the Outer Circle services, was the second of the later pair of Marshall-bodied Reliances, but confusingly entered service in March 1964, some three months after the first identical pair. It is standing alongside St Margaret's bus station in Burley's Way when working on the 79 route. The bus is in its later cream livery, with one maroon band; it was converted in August 1967 to a two-door layout and a reduced seating capacity of B50D. (R. H. G. Simpson)

198 (198 GJF)

Opposite above: The first two of the Marshall-bodied AEC Reliance 4MU3RAs arrived in December 1963 as single-door fifty-four-seaters. 198 (198 GJF) is in Narborough Road as it works on the 91 Outer Circle route. It is in original condition, with cream livery and maroon skirts, window surrounds, and the single front entrance. Being underfloor-engined buses with a large seating capacity, high floor line and quite narrow doorway, Leicester's Marshall-bodied AEC Reliances were not ideal. Loading times were often slow and difficult for the elderly, mothers with small children and/or prams, and anyone laden down with shopping. In August 1967, the four buses were converted to a two-door layout by Strachan to improve accessibility. The bus, along with the remainder of the type, were all withdrawn in October 1971, as they were non-standard. They were replaced and augmented by the influx of the low-floor Metro-Scania single-deckers. The five AEC Reliances were all sold to Colchester Corporation, where they lasted for over five years, ironically rebuilt in the original front-entrance layout. (T. W. Moore)

199 (GBC 199D)

Above: Leaving the garage and turning into Abbey Park Road on Tuesday 17 August 1971 was 199 (GBC 199D), the last of the five AEC Reliance 4MU3RAs with a Marshall B54F body. This bus, although virtually identical to the earlier quartet, was delivered in May 1966; however, this still didn't prevent the bus being withdrawn in October 1971 along with the others, meaning it had only a little over five years' service with Leicester. These were Leicester's first at 36 feet long and 8 feet, 2.5 inches wide, and were all equipped with AEC AH470 engines of 7.57 litres capacity, coupled to a synchromesh manual gearbox. The centre door was fitted immediately in front of the rear axle in August 1967, giving the bus a somewhat ungainly appearance. (M. W. Greenwood)

The PD3/1s, and Other Early 30-Foot-Long Buses

SDU 711

SDU 711 was a Daimler CVG6 demonstrator, built for the 1955 Scottish Commercial Show, and had a Willowbrook H37/29RD body built directly on to the chassis without an underframe. The result was a body that had an overall height of only 14 feet, but retained a 'highbridge' layout with the lower saloon panels below the waistrail becoming noticeably shallower. The bus was fitted with a Twiflex centrifugal clutch, which gave a conventional friction drive but with an automatic engagement, thus giving better fuel economy than a bus with a fluid flywheel. Demonstrated to LCT during October 1956, SDU 711 covered 2,676 miles and averaged 10.17 mpg. Despite its good performance, no orders for the model were placed. It is working on the Southfields Drive service and is standing in Welford Road outside the premises of J. W. Barker & Sons, who were painters and sign writers. (D. R. Harvey Collection)

161 (TBC 161)

On 1 July 1956, an amendment to the British Construction and Use Regulations permitted the operation of two-axle double-deckers up to 30 feet in length. Leyland stretched their successful Titan PD2 chassis, increasing the wheelbase to 18 feet and 6 inches in order to accommodate 30-foot bodywork. The new PD3 used the Leyland o.600 9.8-litre diesel engine found in the PD2, and was a very attractive proposition because it had many of the same chassis components. Leicester Corporation Transport decided to opt for a 41/33 seating layout and stayed with this for all subsequent PD3 deliveries. They initially ordered twelve Leyland PD3/4 models equipped with synchromesh transmission, air brakes and exposed radiators, but the order was later amended to the PD3/1 model, which had the Midland Red style of concealed radiator. Park Royal produced numerically the first three vehicles, which were numbered 161–163, and these were delivered in June and July 1958. The bodies were based on a design drawn up by Crossley Motors and were the only Park Royal bodies to this style delivered to Leicester. 161 (TBC 161) is parked in Abbey Park Road Garage yard on 13 May 1962. (A. D. Broughall)

163 (TBC 163)

Above: By the late 1950s, Leicester was considering the replacement of the wartime high-capacity sixty-four-seater three-axle AEC Renowns of 1939 and 1940, which were coming to the end of their economic lives. Consequently, the advent of the Leyland Titan PD3 chassis type came at an opportune moment. Crossing the junction with Rutland Street, 163 (TBC 163) travels along Granby Street as it goes away from Gallowtree Gate on the 29 route to Stoneygate. The bus is the last of the trio of Park Royal-bodied Leyland Titan PD3/1s and had slightly bilious rose-coloured interior Formica panelling; all the PD3s up to 208 had this colour scheme in both saloons. 163 is in the 1961 cream livery, which it received on 15 February 1963. The Midland Red-style concealed radiator assembly particularly suited the Park Royal bodywork, and the space where the original BMMO badge was located on the front grill was neatly replaced by the Leicester Corporation municipal crest. (A. J. Douglas)

164 (TBC 164)

Opposite above: Willowbrook, the Loughborough-based coachbuilder, was quick off the mark to build 30-foot-long rear-entrance double-deck bodies by building the bodies on the second and third Daimler CVG6/30s in 1956. In 1958, Willowbrook built twenty Leyland Titan PD3/4s for Trent Motor Traction, and the next three it built on the new PD3 chassis were numbered 164 to 166 in the Leicester City Transport fleet. 164 (TBC 164) entered service in July 1958 and, after withdrawal in 1974, has been lovingly preserved by the City of Leicester Museum department. 164 is in Humberstone Gate on Thursday 5 July 1962 when working on the 59 route, and is passing the old City of Leicester Boys' School on the corner of Clarence Street. (M. A. Taylor)

166 (TBC 166)

Above: Travelling into the city centre on the 42 route is 166 (TBC 166), the last of the Willowbrook-bodied Leyland Titan PD3/1s. The bus is passing the arrivals entrance of London Road railway station on Thursday 11 May 1967, nearly four years after this section of London Road had been widened. The bodies on these buses had a considerable family resemblance to that built on SDU 711, the 1956 Daimler CVG6 demonstrator, having deep upper saloon side windows; a rather flat front profile; and, for the first time in the fleet, glass-fibre front and rear domes. This bus was the longest lasting of the Willowbrook-bodied PD3/1s, as it was not withdrawn until February 1975. (Photofives)

171 (TBC 171)

Above: The final livery that was introduced in June 1968 was an all-over cream livery but, with only the two lower maroon bands. The remnants of the beading for the now-abandoned maroon band below the upper saloon windows gives the bus a slightly unfinished and top-heavy appearance that emphasises the rather gaunt lines of the Metro-Cammell Orion bodywork. 171 (TBC 171) a Leyland Titan PD3/1s dating from May 1958, stands outside the Palais de Danse in Humberstone Gate when operating on the 32 route to East Park Road. Later that evening, the Ivor Kennedy Sound would be providing the music for the dancers. (D. R. Harvey Collection)

181 (UJF 181)

Above: Pulling out of the bus-stop parking bay at the Melton Road terminus on 7 November 1959 is 181 (UJF 181), when working on the 32 route. As an experiment to assess the performance of another manufacturer's 30-foot-long double-deckers, six Daimler CSG6/30 chassis were purchased for evaluation purposes. These buses had a Gardner 6LW 8.4-litre engine, coupled to a four-speed David Brown synchromesh gearbox. They were fitted with the wide-fronted version of the 'Manchester-style' concealed radiator, whose sides flared outwards towards the bottom; this was only found on the Daimler 30-foot-long models and the shorter CCG and CSG chassis. The six CSG6/30s had the standard Metro-Cammell Orion H41/33R bodywork but, whereas the early PD3/1s nearly all weighed over 8 tons, the Daimler CSG6/30s had an unladen weight of only 7 tons 13.75 cwt. They were all delivered during July and August 1959. (R. Marshall)

173 (UJF 173)

Opposite below: The next batch of six PD3/1 was numbered 173 to 178, and were also bodied with Metro-Cammell H41/33R bodywork. An alteration to the 1956 Construction and Use Regulations regarding the provision of emergency exits meant that the platform cut-out section in the back panel was deemed to be insufficient for passengers to exit the lower saloon of the bus in the event of an accident. As a result, an emergency-exit window was fitted in the first bay of the lower saloon, a feature that was to become a standard feature on all future 30-foot-long rear entrance half-cab buses. 173 (UJF 173), the first of the six buses delivered in July 1959, is working on the 32 route to East Park Road and is passing the Transport offices in Humberstone Gate in August 1959. (P. Yeomans)

184 (UJF 184)

Above: The Daimler CSG6/30s were some of the first buses in the fleet to be repainted in the cream livery, which possibly suited them better than when applied to the PD3/1s with Midland Red-style concealed radiators. 184 (UJF 184) stands outside the Fleur de Lis public house in Belgrave Gate in September 1966, which was one of a number of traditional city-centre public houses that were demolished in the early 1970s. Although they were used regularly in service during their operational life, the early withdrawal of all the Daimler CSG6/30s occurred in 1971. This was because of the desire to standardise the remaining half-cab bus fleet on the Leyland Titan PD3/1s, and also because the David Brown synchromesh gearbox was not easily mastered by many of the drivers. They disliked them and also found them underpowered when compared to the PD3s. (R. Marshall)

202 (XRY 202)

Above: Crossing Charles Street in Humberstone Gate on 25 July 1970 is 202 (XRY 202). This Leyland Titan PD3/1 is in the final two-maroon-band cream livery, leaving behind the beading for the missing upper crimson band below the upper saloon windows. The Metro-Cammell-bodied bus dated from March 1960, and is working on the 21 service. It has just passed the partially half-timbered old City of Leicester Boys' School, Humberstone Gate. This building had been the home of the Wyggeston Girls' School from 1878 until 1929. Turning into Charles Street is a 1966 Riley Kestrel 1100, while behind the bus is a rear-engined Hillman Imp. (A. D. Broughall)

201 (XRY 201)

Opposite below: With the offside indicator switched on, the driver of 201 (XRY 201) is about to pull away from the stop in front of the Lewis department store in Humberstone Gate. The bus is working on the 29 route to Stoneygate, and is in its original crimson with cream saloon window surrounds. The bus is the first of four Metro-Cammell H41/33R bodied Leyland Titan PD3/1s that had entered service in March 1960. Originally intended to be registered WRY 201, it would later be modified by the fitting of an offside illuminated fluorescent advertisement panel. It would remain in service with Leicester for exactly fifteen years. (B. Coney/R. F. Mack)

205 (XRY 205)

Above: Rounding Parliament Square is the hardly recognisable 205 (XRY 205). This East Lancs-bodied Leyland Titan PD3/1 was the first of the 1975 batch of buses to be withdrawn. Its brief afterlife was 205's claim to fame. After sale along with 202 (XRY 202) and 203 (XRY 203), it was acquired by Guards Coaches of London and they were substantially rebuilt to resemble vintage buses. This was just as sightseeing tours around the capital were beginning. Vehicles such as former-Midland Red BMMO D9 double-deckers – converted to open-top and owned by Prince Marshall's Obsolete Fleet – vied with real or mock vintage buses for this early custom. Former Leicester City Transport 205 was rebuilt in early 1977, when it was given a dummy exposed radiator, an outside staircase and a rebuilt front in the style of a General ST class of 1929. In this guise, it plied its trade for Guards until 1981. (R. F. Mack)

206 (XRY 206)

Opposite above: Travelling along Dun's Lane, which led off West Bridge, and passing the West End Inn, is 206 (XRY 206). It is working on the 52 route. This was a Leyland Titan PD3/1, one of four that were of a batch of buses with two notable features. They were the last Midland Red-fronted Leylands to be delivered to Leicester and were, therefore, the last PD3/1s in the fleet. Conversely, they had bodies built by East Lancashire Coachbuilders of Blackburn, who produced a most attractive, if somewhat heavy, vehicle that weighed 8 tons, 4.5 cwt. The bus was delivered in February 1960 and finished its operational life working for Warrington Borough Council, as their fleet number 6, for two years until 1977. (R. Marshall)

76 MME

Above: In 1958, the fourth AEC Bridgemaster B3RA was demonstrated to Leicester Transport. It was borrowed twice by the Corporation, firstly for just four days between 20 and 23 May 1958, and then for a longer period between 30 June and 15 July 1958. The attractive-looking Park Royal H41/31R bodywork was basically a Crossley design with lightweight alloy framing, and was built only on the first five Bridgemaster prototypes. The demonstration of the integral AEC Bridgemaster must have been successful, as ten of the model were purchased between October 1959 and September 1962. 76 MME is parked in Welford Road during its second loan period on 8 July 1958. (M. A. Sutcliffe)

213 (VJF 213)

Above: The first pair of AEC Bridgemaster B3RAs entered service with Leicester City Transport in October 1959, but 213 and 214 were very different beasts to the demonstrator MME 76. The square-fronted Park Royal body was fitted with fibreglass front and rear domes, and was far less attractive than the body style on MME 76. The B3RA model had the AEC AV 590 9.6-litre engine, which was more than adequate for a bus weighing just a shade over 8 tons. 216 (216 AJF), one of a batch of five buses (215 to 219), cost £6,058 10s 0d. Built on the same chassis-less principle as the Routemaster, the AEC Bridgemaster used AEC front and rear sub frames in order to create an integral, chassis-less vehicle. However, unlike the Routemaster, it did not have power steering and was only offered with a synchromesh gearbox. With a height of only about 13 feet, 5⅝ inches, 213 (VJF 213) is outside the Fleur de Lis public house in Belgrave Gate in its original maroon-and-cream livery. It was repainted into the cream and three-maroon-band livery on 23 November 1962, being the second bus to be repainted in this style. Its twin 214 was the first trail-blazing repaint, done eighteen months earlier on 5 May 1961 for that year's Lord Mayor's Show. (D. R. Harvey Collection)

221 (221 DRY)

Above: The last three of Leicester's ten AEC Bridgemasters had the chassis numbers B3RA162 to 164, which was getting towards the end of the model's total production total of just 179 units. Although LCT had little need for low-height buses, especially a vehicle under 13.5 feet high, the chassis-less Bridgemasters were purchased because of their advanced specification, smooth ride and low, flat floor – although the air suspension on the back axle was sufficiently bouncy to induce seasickness! 221 (221 DRY) runs down Granby Street towards Gallowtree Gate when working on the 42 service. The tall tower above and behind the parked 1959 Standard Ten van belongs to the Grand Hotel just beyond Belvoir Street. (R. Marshall)

217 (217 AJF)

Opposite below: 217 (217 AJF) was bought for preservation by the 217 Preservation Group, and took part in the LTHG Rally at Quorn railway station on 23 April 2016. Looking as it did when brand new in September 1961, with the all-over cream livery and three maroon bands, 217 was repainted twice; once after three years' service in May 1964, and again in August 1968, when it was one of the first to be repainted without the upper maroon band. Originally bought with seventy-two seats, an additional row was inserted in the upper deck in March 1963, which increased capacity to seventy-six. The Bridgemasters had a relatively short life in Leicester, due to being non-standard, and 217 was last used in service on Friday 14 May 1971. It spent most of its post-Leicester life working for a fruit farmer – Peter Arbuckle & Sons of Star Inn Farm, Invergowrie, near Dundee – where it was used to transport farm workers. Eventually it went to Dunsmore of Larkhall, a scrap dealer, in May 1990. 217 was purchased by the Leicester Bridgemaster Group in May 1999 for preservation and, after a twelve-year restoration that included new frames, stress panels, platform and staircase, 217 successfully gained a Class 5 MOT in July 2011. (D. R. Harvey)

248 (248 AJF)

Above: Working on the 18 route in 1962, 248 (248 AJF) rounds the traffic island in Belgrave Gate. This was one of the first Leyland Titan PD3s purchased by Leicester City Transport to be fitted with the new standard St Helen's concealed radiator. This was made of moulded glass fibre, which had a scalloped bonnet top to aid the driver's visibility. The front of the bonnet carried the word 'LEYLAND', a large two-section radiator aperture with horizontal slats to aid cooling and a recessed offside moulding to match the shaped bonnet top. The new bonnet was introduced in 1960 and, on the 30-foot-long Titans for Leicester with synchromesh gearboxes and air brakes, it was designated PD3A/1s. The batch was numbered 245 to 249 and had Metro-Cammell Orion H41/33R bodywork; they were the first in the fleet to have walnut-coloured interior Formica panelling. They weighed 7 tons, 15.5 cwt, which was the lightest of any of Leicester's PD3s. (B. Coney)

252 (252 DRY)

Above: Passing into Gallowtree Gate, with Horsefair Street and the National Provincial Bank on the corner of Granby Street behind it, is bus 252 (252 DRY). It is a Leyland Titan PD3A/1, with an East Lancs H41/33R body and delivered in July 1962; here it is working on the 41 service. The six East Lancs-bodied buses were equipped from new with an offside fluorescent-lit advertisement panel. In the early 1960s, these brightly illuminated signs were briefly very popular, as they brought in extra revenue to the undertaking. Nevertheless, it was soon discovered that they were a mixed blessing, as they drained the batteries on the bus very quickly and were often quite unreliable, with electrical faults leaving the panels half-lit, flickering or just not working! The bus is by now in the cream livery with two maroon bands. (R. Marshall)

249 (249 AJF)

Opposite below: Coming out of Haymarket *c*. 1974 is Leyland Titan PD3A/1 249 (249 AJF), the last of the five Metro-Cammell-bodied buses. Here it is working on the 33 route. The six-storey Haymarket Centre, behind the bus, was opened on 4 June 1973. Along with the AEC Bridgemasters 215 to 219 delivered during the same month, 249 entered service in September 1961; they were the first to enter service in the new cream livery with three maroon bands. The bus is painted in the post-1968 livery that omitted the upper maroon livery band, which always gave the Metro-Cammell-bodied buses a tall, gaunt look. It would remain in service until February 1976, after which it was operated by Whippet Coaches of Fenstanton. (A. Yates)

256 (256 ERY)

Coming into the city centre in Humberstone Gate is one of the ten Park Royal-bodied Leyland Titan PD3A/1s that entered service in January 1963. The Park Royal body fitted to 256 (256 ERY) was a very different design to the first three PD3s delivered to the Corporation in July 1958. The body was built to a new metal-framed design by Park Royal, in which the upper saloon was very similar to the contemporary MCCW Orion bodies, except for the distinctively curved rear dome. With their commodiously wide cabs and windscreen, the front of the body had distinctive vertical front panelling, the Park Royal bodywork weighed 8 tons and 3 qtrs; this made them considerably lighter, by almost 4 cwt, than the PD3s bodied by East Lancs, but a quarter of a ton heavier than the Metro-Cammell bodied examples. The bus is passing the Palais de Danse, with the tall brick-built St James' Building beyond that on the corner of St James Street, above the Austin Mini-Cooper. (A. Richardson)

264 (264 ERY)

Probably the best known of all the Leicester PD3A/1s is 264 (264 ERY). Not only did it operate for many years as the first of Guide Friday's open-top buses in Stratford-upon-Avon, but your author had the misfortune to drive it into the canopy of Stratford railway station, damaging the canopy and the front corner of the nearside upper saloon! It entered service on 12 January 1963 and, after fourteen years of service in Leicester, 264 was withdrawn in October 1977. Bought by Guide Friday, 264's Park Royal body was converted by Willowbrook to its open-top condition and it served Roger Thompson's Guide Friday fleet for over twenty years, straying little from their original operational base around Stratford. After going into semi-retirement, the bus was on loan for display and occasional use at the Aston Manor Road Transport Museum in Birmingham. It was purchased by Leicester Transport Heritage Trust in 2011 and returned to Leicester for continued preservation. It is parked in Henley Street, just beyond the sixteenth-century house that was William Shakespeare's birthplace. (D. R. Harvey)

398 JTB

Above: Manufacturers of PSVs frequently produced a bus for use as a demonstrator, with the aim of impressing enough to get an order. In October 1960, Leyland Motors sent the already sixteen-month-old 398 JTB for assessment by Leicester City Transport. This was Leyland's first production demonstrator rear-engined Atlantean PDR1/1 model, and it was fitted with a Metro-Cammell H44/34F body. In company with a Ford Prefect 100E and a Hillman Minx Series I convertible, 398 JTB, suitably adorned with large Leicester Transport notices in the lower saloon windows, is being used on the 30 service in Evington Road. The driver and conductor are treating the bus as if it were an open-rear platform bus, as it is running with the front doors open. It obviously made a reasonably good impression as, eventually, three Atlanteans were purchased in 1963. After it had completed its time as a demonstrator, it was sold in February 1961 to Scout of Preston, who numbered it 2 in their fleet. (A .J. Douglas)

187 (187 DRY)

Above: 187 (187 DRY), carrying a full load of passengers, turns around the traffic island at the junction of Belgrave Gate and the distant Charles Street on 22 May 1965. This Leyland Atlantean PDR1/1 is working on the 14 New Parks service, and has just overtaken a Midland Red BMMO D7. Like the Leicester bus, this too has a Metro-Cammell body but had a seating capacity that was nineteen fewer. The cream livery with three maroon stripes was well suited to the boxy-shaped MCCW bodywork, and was reputedly derived from the general manager seeing Sheffield Corporation's recently delivered buses in their all-over cream with dark-blue bands. Behind the bus is Danilo Govonis Dany's ladies' hairdressing salon, reputedly the largest ladies' hairdressers in Europe at this time. (R. H. G. Simpson)

185 (185 DRY)

Opposite below: The delivery of the first three Leyland Atlantean PDR1/1s filled in the next vacant fleet numbers, but were chronologically out of sequence as they did not enter service until February 1963. 185 (185 DRY), with a somewhat utilitarian Metro-Cammell H44/33F body, was the first of the trio of rear-engined buses in the fleet, and had the same Leyland 0.600 engine 9.8-litre units, albeit transversely mounted, as the front-engined PD3s. They were purchased to evaluate operating these front-entrance high-capacity vehicles and were fitted with a semi-automatic pneumocyclic gearbox. It is being used on 26 service and is passing the Labour Exchange in Charles Street, with Bedford Street partially hidden by the bus. (A. J. Douglas)

76 (76 HBC)

Above: Waiting outside the old Savoy Cinema in Belgrave Gate is 76 (76 HBC), the first of
the Park Royal H41/33R-bodied Leyland Titan PD3A/1s delivered in April 1964, and by
this time painted in the 1968 two-maroon-banded cream livery. The art deco-styled Savoy
Cinema was built for Associated British Cinemas, and opened on 4 June 1937. It was equipped
with a Compton three-manual organ that, with its illuminated console, survived until 1970,
and the cinema eventually closed on 16 January 1997. In 1973, after the cinema had been
divided into three, it was showing two films, with the main one being *Never Give an Inch*.
This was a none-too-successful 1971 American drama, directed by Paul Newman and starring
Newman, Henry Fonda and Lee Remick. The second film was the 1972 British comedy film
Steptoe and Son, which was a spin-off from the popular British television comedy series
starring Wilfrid Brambell and Harry H. Corbett as the warring father-and-son rag-and-bone
men. (A. J. Douglas)

79 (79 HBC)

Opposite above: Standing empty at the New Parks terminal lay-by of the 14 service is 79
(79 HBC). The bus is showing the 26 destination number to Welford Road at a time when
the New Parks services were being coupled with those going to Welford Road. 79 was one
of the five Leyland Titan PD3A/1s delivered to the Corporation in April 1964 that had Park
Royal H41/33R bodywork. These three Park Royal-bodied buses were again easily identifiable
by their wide driver's cabs and the almost overhanging flat front of the upper saloon. This
style of metal-framed body was inherited from the production AEC Bridgemasters. The bus is
in its original three-band cream livery, but appears to be missing its radiator filler cap on the
St Helens-styled concealed radiator. (D. R. Harvey Collection)

85 (85 HBC)

Above: Parked in front of the main entrance of the Lewis department store in Humberstone Gate is an almost new 85 (85 HBC). This was many years before Humberstone Gate was pedestrianised and buses terminated in the heart of the city centre. The art deco-styled Lewis building was the prestige place to shop in Leicester city centre. The bus, working on the 29 route, is a Leyland Titan PD3A/1 with an East Lancashire H41/33R body, delivered to the Transport Department in March 1964. These buses, with their maple-coloured interior Formica panelling, were both stylish and well-constructed, weighing 8 tons, 4 cwt 3 qtrs. (P. Yeomans)

91 (91 HBC)

Above: John Richardson, who were manufacturing chemists, occupied part of Lillie House, a 1930s building on the corner of London Road and Conduit Street. The long climb up towards the distant Victoria Park can be appreciated from this position at the bottom of the hill. Halfway up the hill, on the right, is the graceful tall tower of the Victoria Road Baptist Church Institute. Built in 1866 in the Gothic style, the church stands on the corner of London Road and Victoria Road, later renamed University Road. The bus is 91 (91 HBC), another of the 1964 East Lancs-bodied Leyland Titan PD3A/1s. It travels into the city centre and is about to pass, on its offside, the southernmost corner of the London Road railway station buildings. 91 is working back to the bus garage at Abbey Park Road, having worked on the 29 Stoneygate service on 22 May 1965. (R. H. G. Simpson)

72 (CJF 72C)

Above: Working on the 25 route in Pocklington's Walk and travelling towards Horsefair Street is 72, (CJF 72C), an East Lancs-bodied Leyland Titan PD3A/1, dating from February 1965. This batch of ten buses, numbered 66 to 75, was the first in the fleet to have saloon heaters, something that helped to push the unladen weight up to 8 tons, 5 cwt, 3 qtrs, making them the heaviest PD3 thus far. Behind the bus is Welford Place, with buildings that were soon to be swept away to make way for the construction of the New Walk Centre. In about 1971, bus 72, now in the two-maroon-band livery, has just overtaken a 1961-registered Volkswagen 1200 Beetle, parked outside the premises of optician E. H. Taylor, as it goes into the city centre. It is noticeable that parking is still being allowed on the one side of the street, a situation that would soon change with increased amounts of traffic. (A. D. Broughall)

66 (CJF 66C)

Opposite below: Just hooking into the nearside lane in order to gain its bus stop is 66 (CJF 66C), the first of the 1965 deliveries of East Lancs-bodied Leyland Titan PD3A/1s, which, in this case, arrived in February of that year. The East Lancs body had a more 'harmonious' appearance than either of the bodies supplied by Metro-Cammell and Park Royal, with less obvious use of glass fibre in the upper saloon. The bus is in Belgrave Gate and has just passed the Hanson's-owned Griffin Inn. The bus is working on the 54 service on 22 May 1965, but bears the somewhat vague destination of 'CENTRE', although the bus was actually terminating in Charles Street. (R. H. G. Simpson)

188 (DBC 188C)

Above: Announced in 1962, the low-floor, double-deck AEC Renown was designed with a chassis and was intended to take over from the integral AEC Bridgemaster. 3B3RA versions had four-speed synchronised gearboxes, and this was the model ordered by Leicester. There were thirteen AEC Renown 3B3RA, of which the first three had forward-entrance bodywork built by East Lancs with a H44/31F seating layout. The first three took the next available fleet numbers and were numbered 188 to 190. The first of these, 188 (DBC 188C), entered service on 26 August 1965. They cost £6,908 each, plus an additional £50 for a 'sunshine' translucent double-skin roof on the top deck. These were very heavy buses, each weighing 8 tons, 16.5 cwt. (D. R. Harvey Collection)

36 (FJF 36C)

Above: The AEC Renown was a replacement for the Bridgemaster, and outwardly looked generally very like that model. Underneath, it differed, as there was a separate chassis, which would hopefully rectify the criticism that the Bridgemaster had lost some sales because of the non-availability of alternative to the standard Park Royal bodywork. A key identification feature was the projection of the offside front mudguard beyond the cab front panel, and the use of an almost-standard version of the Regent V bonnet. Leicester City Transport's 36 (FJF 36C) was the first of ten AEC Renown 3B3RA with East Lancashire H43/31R bodies, and entered service in December 1965. It was the first of the only pair to be registered with C suffixes. The bus is turning right from Granby Street into Halford Street, having just passed the National Westminster Bank, which was occupying the premises of the National Provincial Bank as a result of the merger on 1 January 1970 with the Westminster Bank. The bus is in the post-1968 livery and is working on the 18 service on 23 September 1975. (A. Beech)

189 (DBC 189C)

Opposite below: All the AEC Renown 3B3RAs had deep windows in both saloons on the East Lancashire bodies, giving the buses a strikingly modern appearance. 189 (DBC 189C) travels along Abbey Street towards Burleys Way from Belgrave Gate when working on the very-well-patronised 14 service to New Parks. Behind the bus, which is in the original three-maroon band livery, is the seven-storey Abbey Street multi-storey car park. Following behind the bus is a Ford Corsair 120E four-door saloon. The forward-entrance Renowns had AEC 9.6-litre engines, coupled to a four-speed synchromesh gearboxes with air brakes. The model used independent front suspension and air-bellows rear suspension, which, throughout their lives, caused ride height problems as, when empty and the air bellows were uncompressed, it left the step into the lower saloon rather high for boarding. The final bus of the trio, 190 (DBC 190) is now beautifully restored. (M. Fenton)

41 (FJF 41D)

Above: Still in its original cream with the three-crimson band livery, AEC Renown 3B3RA 41 (FJF 41D), with an East Lancashire H43/31R body, is working on the 36 service. These buses were very heavy for half-cab, front-engined buses, even by the standards of 1966 – weighing some 8 tons 14.75 cwt, which was about three-quarters of a ton more than one of the undertaking's PD3s! The low height of these buses is emphasised by the shallow panels below the lower saloon windows. The Renowns' advanced specification just couldn't compete with such buses, and it hardly looked the part of an up-to-date bus design for the swinging sixties. It was therefore not surprising that the Renown was only marginally more successful that the Bridgemaster with a total of only 251 being built between 1962 and 1967. It has just passed the premises of Freeman, Hardy & Willis in Granby Street and is being followed by a brave soul learning to drive on a Ford Popular 103E, with its three-speed gearbox, side valve engine, cart suspension and vacuum-operated single windscreen wiper. (R. F. Mack)

46 (GRY 46D)

Opposite above: On a wet, miserable day, climbing up the hill in London Road is 46 (GRY 46D), the first of the April 1966 deliveries received from MCW, entering service on 11 May 1966. 46 (GRY 46D), with its direction indicator still on, is one of the standard Leyland Titan PD3A/1s with seventy-four-seater bodywork, and was the first bus to have what became the standard grey Formica interior finish. It is still in its originally styled three-maroon band livery, which helped to disguise the different depths of the lower and upper saloon windows. The bus is working on the 67 service to Evington and is being followed by a rear-engined Hillman Imp and a Ford Anglia 105E. (R.Marshall)

50 (GRY 50D)

Above: Passing a wonderfully varied collection of differing architecturally styled Victorian villas in London Road is 50, (GRY 50D), a Metro-Cammell-bodied Leyland Titan PD3A/1, dating from June 1966. On Saturday 15 May 1980, a pleasantly sunny spring day and about a fortnight before its withdrawal, 50 is being used on the 29 route, and wears the two-maroon-band livery introduced in 1968. The bus is opposite Victoria Park as it travels out of the city centre, near to the junction with Mayfield Road. The 69-acre park had been Leicester's horse-racing track from 1806 to 1883, and had occupied the former medieval common land known as South Field. The park was opened in 1882, and these houses in London Road were very prestigious as they overlooked the level open grassland and the arboreal delights of the large open space. (A. P. Newland)

52 (GRY 52D)

Above: The inspector gives the bus driver some information as he stands against the nearside front wing of the bus. The bus is at a temporary bus stop in Western Boulevard, alongside the railings that separate the road from the Leicestershire & Northamptonshire Union Canal, which was completed in 1810. Western Boulevard was within easy walking distance of the nearby Filbert Street, home of Leicester City FC, and about half a mile away from Leicester Tigers Rugby Ground at Welford Road. As a result, on Saturday afternoons and other match days, Western Boulevard was used to park both buses and coaches usually owned by independent operators, who had brought fans to the games. 52 (GRY 52D), a MCW-bodied Leyland Titan PD3A/1, is working on the 49 route on Saturday 21 April 1979, and is in Western Boulevard on a route diversion, due to the proximity that day of a National Front rally. (A. P. Newland)

61 (GRY 61D)

Above: Park Royal-bodied Leyland Titan PD3A/1 61 (GRY 61D) stands at a bus stop in Uppingham Road. It is working on the 61 service on 26 September 1980, just beyond Overton Road. The wide windscreen, the flat front and the slightly bulbous shape of the upper saloon were distinctive features of the Park Royal metal-framed bodywork, which was emphasised by the omission of the upper maroon band. The deep lower saloon windows, coupled with the much shallower ones in the upper saloon, seemed almost to copy the Orion body produced by Metro-Cammell. The more rectangular shape of the front dome ventilator was most distinctive, as other manufacturer's bodies employed a much more square design. (A. P. Newland)

58 (GRY 58D)

Opposite below: Parked at the entrance to Haymarket, with the Clock Tower and East Gates behind it, is a rather dust-covered 58 (GRY 58D) in its final cream livery with two maroon bands. The bus is working on the 42 service to Melton Road in August 1980, just two months before it was withdrawn. 58 is a Park Royal-bodied Leyland Titan PD3A/1 that entered service in September 1966. Once again, the weight of these ten buses had crept up to 8 tons, 1 cwt, making them the heaviest of any of the Park Royal-bodied PD3A/1s. To the left of the Clock Tower is Gallowtree Gate. The Clock Tower was constructed in 1868 at a cost of just over £2,000. Officially a memorial, the Clock Tower was built to become a focal point in the centre of Leicester. It has four corner-mounted statues, each made from Portland stone. The figures are all historically important in the history of Leicester; they are Simon de Montfort (1208–1265), William Wyggeston (c. 1497–1586), Sir Thomas White (1492–1567) and Gabriel Newton (1683–1762). (D. R. Harvey)

16 (LJF 16F)

Above: The last deliveries to Leicester City Transport of Leyland Titan PD3s looked superficially like many of the earlier ones. However, there was one major difference. All of the twenty 1967 deliveries were the PD3/12 model, which had Leyland's pneumocyclic semi-automatic gearbox. In 1967, Leyland Motors dropped the A chassis type designation for buses equipped with the St Helens-style concealed radiator and bonnet assembly; therefore, these buses were not strictly PD3As. The ten East Lancs-bodied buses were numbered 16 to 25, and were up to the usual attractive standard of that company's bodywork. However, they did weigh the heaviest of all Leicester's PD3s, tipping the scales at 8 tons, 8 cwt. 16 (LJF 16F), working on the 18 service, turns to cross the Clock Tower junction from Humberstone Gate into East Gate in early 1973. Following the bus are a Wolseley 1500 and a Morris Oxford VI saloon. This bus was saved for preservation initially by LCT, but sadly was lost during October 2011 in an arson attack on a nearby barn. (A. D. Broughall)

25 (LJF 25F)

Opposite above: Loading up with passengers in Humberstone Gate on the corner with Hill Street is 24 (LJF 24F). The bus is working the 61 service to Nether Hall. 25 was a Leyland Titan PD3/12 with an East Lancashire H41/33R body that entered service in October 1967, and is in the cream livery with two maroon bands. Behind it is 287 (GJF 287N), a Metro-Cammell-bodied Metropolitan with Scania BR111DH, which was barely eight years younger than the PD3/12. Bus design had moved on in those few years, but the failings of the Metropolitans included excessive body corrosion problems and a fuel consumption rate that was bordering on the desperate. Consequently, the two-pedal control, semi-automatic Leyland might have been considered to be a better investment, even if the open-platform half-cab double-decker was an old-fashioned concept. (R. Marshall)

26 (LJF 26F)

Above: Not every bus sold goes to an independent operator to live out its dotage, pottering about the byways of England or Scotland. Occasionally, a bus is found useful for a quite unusual purpose and even in a quite distant field. The first of the MCW-bodied Leyland Titan PD3/12s was 26 (LJF 26F), which entered service with Leicester City Transport in December 1967, and was withdrawn in February 1982, whence it was sold to the Castle Point Bus Company of Benfleet. On 27 October 1999, within 2 miles of the site of the Battle of Waterloo – famous for the Duke of Wellington's victory over Napoleon Bonaparte on June 18, 1815 – Leicester's former 26 was being used as a playbus next to a McDonald's hamburger restaurant. (D. R. Harvey)

30 (LJF 30F)

Above: A well-loaded lower saloon and a virtually empty upper deck seems to be usual for double-deck operation out of the peak periods in Leicester. Waiting in Charles Street, 30 (LJF 30F), one of the ten Leyland Titan PD3/12s with MCW H41/33R delivered in December 1967, is working on the 53 service on 1 June 1968. The seven-month-old bus is in its original three-maroon-band cream livery. All of these last PD3s were equipped with offside fluorescent advertisement panels, with bus 30 having an advertisement for the first Woolco department store, which was an up-market version of F. W. Woolworth, its parent company. (G. Mead)

1 (LJF 1F)

Above: Coming out of Humberstone Gate when working on the 20 service is the first of the Bristol RESL6Ls with ECW B42D bodywork. 1 (LJF 1F) entered service in October 1967, at the same time the East Lancs PD3/12s were arriving and providing a stark contrast between the traditional and the new. The Bristol single-deckers were equipped for pay-as-you-enter operation, and were used on the short-lived Centre Circle route. The RESL6L model was 32-feet, 6-inches long and had a rear-mounted horizontal Leyland 0.600 9.8-litre engine with a semi-automatic gearbox. The whole of this batch were withdrawn on 1 November 1978 and sold to Blackburn Borough Council. (A. J. Douglas)

32 (LJF 32F)

Opposite below: Pulling across the carriageway lanes in Burleys Way, alongside the western end of St Margaret's bus station, is 32 (LJF 32F). The bus, a MCW-bodied Leyland Titan PD3/12, is working on the 14 route in 1975. These buses had the usual lightweight Orion bodywork that weighed 7 tons, 19 cwt, 3 qtrs, some 8 cwt lighter than the corresponding East Lancashire-bodied buses delivered earlier in 1967. The MCW body had already been in production for over twelve years, and was an attempt to reduce weight – and, therefore, fuel consumption – at a time when passenger numbers were beginning to fall. Consequently, the Orion body always looked sparse and slightly out of proportion, although liveries such as Leicester's did somewhat disguise any ungainliness in the design. Following the bus are two different models of Ford Cortina – Marks II and III – and a Morris Marina, while on the opposite side of the road is a Vauxhall Viva HC. (D. R. Harvey Collection)

5 (LJF 5F)

Above: 5 (LJF 5F), the last of the ECW-bodied Bristol RESL6Ls of 1967, crosses Humberstone Gate as it travels along Charles Street when working on the Centre Circle 44 route. This was the service for which these buses were intended. These ECW-bodied buses had a flat front and shallow windscreen, which was matched by the very square rear end and an emergency door in the rear panel. This was in marked contrast to the RESL6Ls delivered to nearby Coventry Corporation in February 1967, which had the first style of bodywork with a very rounded rear dome. Coming out of Humberstone Gate is a Jaguar 3.4-litre Mark I on trade plates and a Ford Zephyr 4 Mark III saloon. Behind the bus on the corner of Charles Street and Humberstone Gate is a typical 1930s art deco block of shops. (T.W.Moore)

97 (PBC 97G)

Above: Some of the first Leyland Atlantean PDR1A/1s to receive Eastern Counties bodywork were supplied to LCT. Entering service on 1 January 1969, 97 (PBC 97G), the second of the first ten of these Atlanteans, turns out of Carisbrooke Road into Knighton Road when working on the 57 route in July 1974. These second generation of Leicester's Atlanteans had the large 11.1-litre 0680 Power Plus Leyland engine. The ECW bodies were based on the design for the new rear-engined, front-entrance Bristol VR type. By 1968, this body style was modified again in order to suit the vagaries of the Daimler Fleetline and the Leyland Atlantean chassis. The first orders for non-Bristol chassis ECW-bodied double-deckers came from Coventry Corporation, with eighteen Daimler Fleetlines CRG6LXs in April 1968, and from Leicester City Transport for ten Leyland Atlantean chassis eight months later. These were the first new buses delivered in the all-over cream livery, but only with the lower and extremely thick maroon bands. (D. R. Harvey Collection)

8 (PBC 8G)

Opposite below: Three more of the Bristol RE/ECW combination arrived in October and November 1968, and were numbered 6 to 8. These were the 36-foot-long RELL6L model and had an ECW body, which could accommodate forty-two passengers and had two doors. The extra length of theses buses was emphasised by the seven small saloon windows. They were equipped with the horizontal version of the 9.8-litre Leyland 0.600 engine coupled to a semi-automatic gearbox. 8 (PBC 8G) travels along Granby Street on 23 September when working on the 15 route, and is at the junction with Horsefair Street, marked by the late-Victorian National Westminster Bank building. (MB Transport Photographs)

102 (PBC 102G)

Above: About to cross Humberstone Gate when travelling southwards in Charles Street is ECW-bodied Leyland Atlantean PDR1A/1 102 (PBC 102G), in the Leicester City Transport fleet. The original order for this batch of buses was intended to be another twenty Leyland Titan PD3/12s with, uniquely, a rear-entrance ECW body, based on the style of those latterly fitted to Bristol Lodekka FL chassis. By 1968, the Lodekka chassis was being phased out in favour of the rear-engined VRT model and, in the last year of production, was only built as the forward-entrance FLF type. ECW would have had to build a body considerably modified to suit the Leyland Titan. About the time that the body order contract had been agreed on 31 May 1967, the Labour government had proposed the Transport Act, which was implemented in 1968. One of the main aims of the Act was the provision that new buses should be suitable for one-man operation, and those vehicles that conformed to the legislation were to be eligible for a government subsidy of 25 per cent. Thus the provisional order for an ECW-bodied PD3 was killed off, as there would be no 'bus-grant' funding for such a vehicle, and this tantalising order was cancelled. Leicester therefore got its Leyland/ECW combination, but it arrived as ten Atlanteans, suitable for one-man operation as per the Transport Act. (D. R. Harvey Collection)

106 (PBC 106G)

Opposite above: Turning onto Burleys Way from Abbey Street in July 1972 is 106 (PBC 106G), the first of the Leyland Atlantean PDR1A/1s with Park Royal H43/31F bodywork, which had entered service in April 1969. The 1969 class of ten Park Royal-bodied Leyland Atlanteans had a more up-to-date frontal appearance, originally introduced on a demonstrator in 1965, with the latest style of large V-shaped windscreen and front upper saloon windows of a similar design. The new front-end design of this batch was quite startling, as the new-style upper saloon front windows looked as though they had been inspired by the Christopher Dodson bodies ordered in about 1932 by a few of the London 'pirate' bus operators. (D. R. Harvey Collection)

109 (PBC 109G)

Above: In May 1961, Mr John Cooper, Leicester's general manager, was on a visit to Sheffield Transport, and saw their cream livery with three blue bands. On the strength of that visit, he decided to adopt a triple-maroon-banded cream livery for Leicester. In the mid-1960s, Sheffield Transport purchased a large number of the same Atlantean/Park Royal combination, which were very similar to the ten PBC–G batch that entered service in Leicester during April 1969. One of the little ironies that occasionally occur was when, in the spring of 1981, South Yorkshire PTE had issues over maintenance, resulting in a number of buses being hired from other operators. Six of the Leicester Park Royal-bodied Leyland Atlantean PDR1A/1s with Park Royal bodies went on loan, along with four of the earlier ECW-bodied Atlanteans, in a period starting on 26 March and lasting until 25 June of that year. This included 109 (PBC 109G), thus continuing the appearance of former Sheffield buses in the guise of the ones on loan from the East Midlands. It is in Waingate on 7 April 1981. (P. Yeomans)

112 (PBC 112G)

Above: Showing off its offside illuminated advertisement panel, which was carried by all the
Park Royal-bodied Leyland Atlantean PDR1A/1s, 112 (PBC 112G) stands at the loading stop
in Charles Street on 16 August 1969, having worked on the 62 service into the city centre.
The advertisement for Dulite wallpaper paste was most unusual on buses, being more usually
associated with television adverts. On this warm summer's day, with most of the saloon windows
wide open, the driver of the bus lounges in his cab as he talks with his conductor. The bus
had only recently entered service in April 1969 and, although withdrawn in October 1982, it
remained in service as a driver-training vehicle with the fleet number 412. (A. A. Cooper)

130 (TRY 130H)

Above: Working along Belvoir Street going into Welford Place, and with the Central Lending Library behind it, is 130 (TRY 130H). The ECW body was a very multi-windowed affair, but this increased rigidity and helped to ensure that these Bristol RELL6Ls had long lives. This was coupled to the already sound reputation of the chassis, which was undoubtedly the best of the 1960s generation of rear-engined bus chassis. The contemporary single-deck buses with rear engines were designed to have two-step entrances and a reasonably flat floor towards the front of the rear axle. The previous underfloor-engined chassis, such as the AEC Reliance or Leyland Tiger Cub, both of which were in operation in Leicester, had a positive mountain of entrance steps to negotiate before the saloon level was reached. So, with a relatively low floor line, the new generation of rear-engined single-deckers seemed to be an operator's dream. Unfortunately, they quickly gained unenviable reputations, having problems with body structures failing due to the added weight of the rear-mounted engines; overheating; poor engine reliability; and, in one case, just an appallingly unsuitable engine. The RELL soldiered on and, while not the most sophisticated vehicle in that sandwich box, it was reliable and reasonably trouble free. (A. P. Newland)

120 (TRY 120H)

Opposite below: The second batch of ECW-bodied Bristol RELL6Ls amounted to twenty buses, numbered 116 to 135. Superficially the same as 6–8, the first noticeable difference was the much deeper windscreen that was extended into the front dome. This was narrower and, for the first time, had provision for a three-track number blind. As with the previous trio, they had a centre exit door and provision for forty-seven passengers but, at 7 tons, 13 cwt, 1 qtr, they were almost 2 cwt heavier than the first batch. This was compensated for through equipping them with the larger 11.1-litre Leyland 0.680 engine. Standing in Charles Street in about 1978 is 120 (TRY 120H), which had been delivered in December 1969. It would have almost eleven years working in Leicester before being sold to Ipswich Borough Transport, who operated it as their fleet number 120 for another eight years. (D. R. Harvey)

131 (TRY 131H)

The advantages of the front entrance having two shallow steps were appreciated on the ECW dual-doored Bristol RELL6Ls. It allowed for buses such as 131 (TRY 131H) to unload quickly through the centre door, while easily loading up through the front door without having to negotiate a steep flight of steps – therefore making buses more accessible and available for a wider range of potential passengers. The TRY–H batch of Bristols was not fitted with sliding saloon windows as with the original three, but these buses had prominent rear-mounted air scoops on the rear dome in order to allow more fresh air into the bus, and therefore recirculate the air inside the saloon. The bus is passing The Eclipse public house in East Gates and is being followed by an Austin 1300GT saloon. (A. J. Douglas)

Into the 1970s with New Designs

147 (WBC 147J)

In 1969, the Swedish chassis manufacturer Scania-Vabis and the British company Metro-Cammell Weymann entered into a joint venture to build a new range of technically advanced buses. It involved engines and mechanical units being manufactured in Sweden and then transported to Britain, where they were incorporated with the vehicle's structural components and bodywork at MCW's Birmingham plant. The single-decker came first, with demonstrators appearing in 1969 and the first production buses completed by 1970. However, production only lasted until 1974, with a total of just 133 being built. 147 (WBC 147J) was one of the first eighteen Metro-Scania BR11MHs and entered service in May 1971. The MCW-bodied B44D body was lettered with the commemorative '1952 SILVER JUBILEE 1977' legend on the maroon waistband, which it received in April 1977. It is passing the Swiss Cottage Restaurant in Charles Street when working the 22 route on 21 May 1977. (M. W. Greenwood)

150 (WBC 150J)

Above: Passing The Magazine or Newarke Gateway is MCW-bodied Metro-Scania BR11MH 150 (WBC 150J). It is in Newarke Street, and is travelling towards Welford Place. The Gateway is a Grade I listed building, built in about 1410 by the third Earl of Leicester, and was the entrance into the Newark and Leicester Castle. It was through the archway that, on 21 August 1485, King Richard III emerged as he went to Bosworth, where he was defeated by Henry Tudor. In the English Civil War, it was used to store munitions – hence its present name. The Metro-Scania bus was a fully integral construction, with separate front and rear axle sub-frames. The rear-mounted engine was the Scania D II, a naturally aspirated 11.1-litre six-cylinder diesel unit driving through a fully automatic gearbox. The model was briefly in competition with the newly developed Leyland National and had a reputation of being very fast but heavy on fuel. Leicester, with thirty-five, had the second largest number of Metro-Scania BR111MHs after Newport Corporation. Many were later repainted in the new livery of red, white and grey, which had been introduced in September 1984. (A. J. Douglas)

10 (KHB 186L)

Opposite above: In King Richard's Road on Saturday 5 April 1980 is 10 (KHB 186L), working on the 34 Goodwood route. This was a second-hand purchase from Merthyr Tydfil Corporation, who had two very late Metro-Scanias delivered in April 1973. Numbered 186 and 187, both were sold early in 1979. Leicester acquired 186 in March 1979 via C. F. Booth, the Rotherham dealer. It was initially given the fleet number 10, but was renumbered 208 in February 1981 – the fleet number before those of the second group of seventeen Metro-Scania BR111MHs delivered in late 1971. It was intended to replace the accident-damaged 225, but this bus was eventually repaired, and the former Merthyr Tydfil bus was converted to a dual-purpose layout. The Metro-Cammell bodywork on the single-deck Metro-Scanias was closely based on Scania's own bodywork design, which originally had featured a curved windscreen. However, the resultant extra length made it longer than the then-current British Construction and Use Regulations. The design was altered accordingly, with a flat front and the characteristic asymmetrical windscreen, the nearside one being deeper in order to assist the driver's vision when at a bus stop. (A. P. Newland)

225 (ARY 225K)

Above: The last of the Metro-Scania BR111MH single-deckers, 225 (ARY 225K), is parked in Charles Street outside Safeway's supermarket for a publicity photograph in 1974. This bus had been exhibited at the 1972 Commercial Motor Show as the 'Hush Bus', as it had a package of noise-reducing extras, taking the noise level of the bus down to only 77 decibels. The bus, at 8 tons 13 cwt, was over 5 cwt heavier than the rest of the Corporation's Metro-Scanias because of the extra soundproofing. In addition to the bodywork corrosion, mechanically the powerful Scania 11.1-litre engine was very thirsty and expensive to maintain, while the air suspension was prone to failure, often leaving buses running at strange angles with one side sagging and another angled upward. Yet Leicester managed to overcome most of these difficulties, improving the original fuel consumption up to 5.5 mpg from the appalling 3.2 mpg it managed when first delivered. (M. W. Greenwood)

272 (PJF 272M)

Above: The PJF-registered MCW Metropolitan Scania BR111DHs for Leicester were the second and fourth to the tenth of the type to be built. 272 (PJF 272M) was the ninth, arriving in May 1974. The Metropolitan double-decker was developed from the single-deck Metro-Scania and employed the more powerful 11.1-litre Scania D11CO6 engine with a quiet bus package. Leicester City Transport's general manager, Mr Leslie Smith, must have been impressed with the specification of these modern double-deckers. The municipality was the fourth largest operator of the Metropolitan, with sixty-eight bought new. These powerful buses were popular with the drivers as they were warm, comfortable and fast, as well as being equipped for one-man operation. When still quite new, 272 is parked in front of Abbey Park Road Garage. Through the open front door, the two-step entrance leads to a flat-floored lower saloon. The extensive use of aluminium beading on both sides of the maroon livery band was continued from the single-deck Metro-Scania, as were the nearside and offside radiator grills in front of the rear axle. (P. M. Photography)

303 (GJF 303N)

Opposite above: 303 (GJF 303N) entered service in February 1975, and is working on a route diversion on the 25 route in Bonners Lane, with Oxford Street in the distance, on 21 April 1979. These MCW Metropolitan Scania BR111DHs had MCW H45/28D bodies, which made the total unladen weight very heavy, at a fraction over 10 tons. The body design was a curious mixture, with what was virtually a London Transport DMS upper saloon mounted on a shortened version of the Metro-Scania single-deck bodywork. The whole vehicle was very technically advanced, and initially sales were excellent, with a total of 663 being built. Despite the problems with the steel bodywork corroding, the Leicester Metropolitans had longer lives than Metropolitans had with many other operators. Nevertheless, it is perhaps significant that the replacement MCW Metrobus I was not really favoured, with only four being purchased with similar-looking Metro-Cammell bodies in 1980, and five in 1983 with Alexander bodies. (A. P. Newland)

153 (KJD 206P)

Above: London Transport purchased 164 Metropolitans in 1976, and they became the MD class. Initial mechanical problems with the Scania-engined Metropolitan were largely overcome, but corrosion became an issue that was less easy to solve, resulting in a short eight-year life in London. Former LT fleet number MD6 eventually arrived in Leicester via Trathen Culturebus of Brentford by October 1985, and was numbered, perhaps unusually, 153. This number had been used until the previous year by the single-deck WBC 153J, which had been sold to Leicester City Council for a range of promotional and campaign duties. Leicester eventually acquired five of the former London MD class, which were numbered 282, 149–151 and 153. 153 is in Green Lane Road, working into the city centre on 9 October 1986 on the short-lived Evington service, and is in the 1984 red, white and grey livery. (A. P. Newland)

164 (LNR 164P)

MCW Metropolitan Scania BR111DH 164 (LNR 164P) travels along Downing Drive in Evington as it passes Ingarsby Drive on its offside on 8 October 1986. The bus is working on the 25 route and is by now displaying the prominent 'Leicester City Bus' fleet name on the front panel above the destination box. This bus went on loan to South Yorkshire PTE in June 1976, when it was just three months old, and given the temporary fleet number 589. Just visible on the roof of the front dome is the large fleet number, which was used for bus identification purposes in the garage and in the city centre. 164 was an early withdrawal in April 1988, after being damaged in an accident. (A. P. Newland)

176 (UFP 176S)

Except for an order from Reading Transport for twelve buses, the five UFP-registered buses for Leicester, delivered in October 1977, were the last MCW Metropolitan Scania BR111DHs to be built. They were the only single-door versions operated by the undertaking, and had a rather conservative seating layout of H44/31F. Painted in the red, grey and white livery, 176 (UFP 176S) stands in Church Hill outside the thirteenth-century Church of All Saints, Scraptoft, on 6 September 1985, when being employed on the Polytechnic 41 service. On the side of the bus is an advertisement for Leicester City Bus's new service to the 1950s municipal housing estate at Thurnby Lodge, south of Scraptoft Lane, which, by the late 1980s, had expanded with new housing and required further public transport. (A. P. Newland)

1970s and 1980s Demonstrators

7517 UA

7517 UA was a Roe H38/32R-bodied Daimler CVG6LX that had been new in 1959 to Leeds City Transport as their 517. It was bought by Hestair-Dennis of Guildford in August 1975, who used it as a test-bed for a Voith automatic gearbox coupled to a Gardner 6LXB 10.45-litre engine, which was to be used in the new rear-engined Dennis Dominator chassis. Painted in a biscuit-brown and white livery for use as a demonstrator, it was on loan to Leicester from 7 January 1976 until 7 April 1976, whereupon it was returned to Hestair-Dennis. The interest of Mr Geoffrey Hilditch, the general manager, in the Dominator project and the successful trial with 7517 UA, led to the subsequent purchase of 118 of this new rear-engined bus from Hestair-Dennis. 7517 UA returned to Leicester when it was purchased in January 1978 for spares. It is working on the 29 route in Gallowtree Gate on 15 January 1976. (D. A. Hollingworth)

615 (MAU 615P)

Two buses were on loan from Nottingham Transport, MAU 615P being the first. This was a Leyland Atlantean AN68/1R with an East Lancs H47/31D body, designed to meet Nottingham's exacting, if somewhat idiosyncratic, specifications, and built in December 1975. It was 615 in the Nottingham fleet, and was on loan for just seven days from 17 May to 23 June 1976. It is in Humberstone Gate on 21 May 1976, and is working on the 29 service to Stoneygate. The other bus was a Daimler Fleetline CRG6LX, with a similar-looking body built by Northern Counties, but this was in Leicester for just five days. Neither bus seemed to meet the requirements of LCT, and no orders for either chassis type were ever made, as the new Dennis Dominator was preferred in the Geoffrey Hilditch regime. (M. W. Greenwood)

115 (OCO 115S)

Above: The Leyland Atlantean AN68A/1R had been in production for six years when Plymouth City Transport's 115 (OCO 115S) was borrowed for assessment purposes. It was on loan from 20 March 1978 until 20 May 1978 and, in many ways, was the least adventurous of the borrowed buses demonstrated to LCT in the late 1970s. OCO 115S had a Roe H43/28D body, with the front panel design developed by Park Royal and used on buses delivered to London Country Buses. It is standing alongside Leicester's own 115 (PBC115G) on 18 May 1978, in order to record the coincidence of the recurring 115 fleet number theme. (M. W. Greenwood)

265 (MUT 265W)

Above: In 1980, Scania launched its own double-deck chassis with a transverse 11-litre Scania DN engine; this was the BR112DH, Scania's replacement for the MCW Metropolitan after the joint venture with Metro-Cammell ended. MUT 265W was based with the Gibson of Barlestone fleet, and given the temporary fleet number of 265. The bus had an East Lancs body with a high capacity of H49/37F, and was in a very striking pale-blue livery. MUT 265W entered service on 22 November 1980 and was demonstrated from 2 March 1981 until 16 March 1981 to Nottingham City Transport. MUT 265W is loading up for its first journey on the 23 service to Market Bosworth for the Gibson Division of Citybus. (B. P. A. Garrah)

381 (LWP 381P)

Opposite above: The 139th Ailsa-Volvo B55 to be built was LWP 381P, new to South Yorks PTE in June 1976 as their 381, being one of a batch comprising some sixty-two vehicles. These buses had a front-mounted engine, which still allowed a front-entrance position suitable for one-person operation. It was fitted with the Volvo TD70, turbocharged 6.7-litre engine, coupled to a Self-Changing Gears semi-automatic gearbox. The rest of the design was relatively simple, with beam axles and leaf springs. It had a Van Hool McArdle H44/31D body, built in part of the former CIE Works in Dublin; its design was quite startling, with deep front windows, large upper and lower saloon windows, a front entrance and central exit door. Unfortunately, the body structure was to prove quite frail and VHMA bodies were neither long lived nor well regarded. LWP 381P has the 'on hire to Leicester Transport' notice in the bottom of the nearside windscreen as it turns from Humberstone Gate into Gallowtree Gate; it is working on the 29 service to Stoneygate on Sunday 25 July 1976. It was on loan from 18 July to 1 August 1976, and was used mainly on the 29 and 41 services. (M. W. Greenwood)

XPD 659Y

Standing outside the Fountain public house in Humberstone Gate in September 1982 is the Dennis Falcon V DDA 402 demonstrator XPD 659Y. This bus had an East Lancs H45/37F body, and dated from August 1982. Only six double-decker Falcon Vs were built, and two of these, also with East Lancs bodywork, became Nottingham Corporation's 396 and 397. The other three went to Greater Manchester PTE, with Northern Counties bodies, in the spring of 1984. The Dennis chassis had a powerful, if fairly unusual, Mercedes-Benz 10.96-litre V6 power plant, mounted longitudinally behind the short wheelbase. XPD 659Y, carrying a two-tone green livery, was demonstrated to LCT from 15 September to 4 October 1982. By January 1984, its fairly unsuccessful demonstrating life was over and it was sold to Stevenage Borough as a playbus. After many years as an unused static classroom, it was acquired in 2014 by the Leicester Tram 31 Group for preservation. (B. P. A. Garrah)

Dennis Dominators and Beyond

SHE 722S

The first Dennis Dominator demonstrator arrived in Leicester in November 1977. It was in the livery of South Yorkshire PTE and was registered SHE 722S, although it did not have its allotted 522 fleet number. It was a DD101 model and had an East Lancs H45/32F body. The chassis had a transversely mounted Gardner 6LXB 10.45-litre engine, and was coupled to the same Voith transmission that was fitted to 7517 UA, the ex-Leeds Daimler CVG6 that had run in Leicester during the early part of 1976. With the front door open, the two-step entrance is revealed, which allowed for a flat floor line in most of the lower saloon. The bus was never operated in service, but was used to show what the impending new order would look like. (M. W. Greenwood)

233 (UFP 233S)

Above: When Geoffrey Hilditch was appointed Leicester's general manager, he wanted to purchase Daimler Fleetline chassis, but was informed by Leyland Motors that the model was no longer available. On a take-it-or-leave-it basis, he was told that only Atlanteans were obtainable. As a result of this rebuttal, Mr Hilditch approached Dennis to develop a new rear-engined double-decker bus with an updated Fleetline specification. Mr Hilditch was particularly keen to develop a bus with a radiator located at the front of the chassis instead of on the offside of the engine compartment, as per the Leyland Atlantean or Daimler Fleetline chassis, while utilising the Voith fully automatic gearbox, fitted with a built-in retarder. The first Dominator to be completed for Leicester was the second chassis to be constructed. East Lancs H44/33F-bodied 233 (UFP 233S) was delivered on 26 October 1977; the launch of the new bus in Leicester was at the Abbey Park Road Garage two days later. Several elderly Dennis buses were in attendance, including the 1929 West Bromwich EA 4181 Dixon-bodied Dennis E, just visible behind the brand new Dominator; and, in General livery, the former Dominion 4-ton Dennis XX 9591, with a Dodson O24/24RO body dating from 1925. A sparkling 233 is parked in the garage on 28 October 1977, just before being driven on a short tour of the city by the general manager. (D. R. Harvey)

231 (UFP 231S)

Opposite above: Marshalls of Cambridge built only a comparatively small number of double-deck bodies, ten being on Dennis Dominator: seven for Leicester and three for Derby. Additionally, over a four-year period, they built twenty-eight Scania BR112 H chassis for Newport Corporation; twenty-five for South Yorkshire PTE on Leyland Atlantean AN68/1R chassis; and ten on Leyland Olympian chassis for Bournemouth Yellow Bus in 1982. 231 (UFP 231S) and 232 (UFP 232S) are parked waiting for the handing over ceremony at the eighteenth-century-style White House Hotel, Scraptoft, on 8 June 1978, prior to delivery to LCT. The body design was an uncomfortable mix of contrasting styles, with the rather bulbous windscreen area and slab-sided lower saloon contrasting with the inward crank of the upper saloon windows, which was further emphasised by the oddly shaped pair of front windows. 231 was used as a demonstrator from November to December 1978 by Tayside Regional Council. (M. W. Greenwood)

203 (YRT 203T)

Above: Turning from Gallowtree Gate into Humberstone Gate is 203 (YRT 203T), a Dennis Dominator DD110 with an East Lancs H43/33F body. The bus is heading for the city terminus of the 41 route. This body design was very popular and could claim its origins in the buses built to the specification of Bolton Corporation's general manager, Mr Ralph Bennett, and delivered in April 1963. This bus had entered service in January 1979, but was unfortunate enough to be severely damaged in an accident in August 1986, resulting in it becoming withdrawn and stripped for spares at Abbey Park Road Garage. (M. W. Greenwood)

36 (FUT 36V)

Unlike the MCW Metropolitan Scania, which was a regular double-deck purchase by LCT from 1974 until 1977, its successor, the MCW Metrobus, was all but ignored by the undertaking. The typical MCW-bodied Mark I Metrobus only received one small order for just four buses, which were numbered 36 to 39. 36 (FUT 36V) has just passed HMP Leicester in Welford Road on the right on 22 April 1989. The prison was designed by Leicester county surveyor William Parsons to resemble a castle, and cost £20,000 by the time it was opened in 1828. Attached to one of the un-castellated towers is a security camera; the gatehouse, including the adjoining buildings to the north and south, and the perimeter wall are Grade II listed. On the left, with Infirmary Road forking to the left beyond it, is the Victorian children's hospital. 36 is working on the 38 route and is in a slightly modified CityBus livery, which lacks the white relief below the lower deck windows. (A. P. Newland)

250 (FUT 250V)

250 (FUT 250V), a Dennis Dominator DDA120 with an East Lancs H44/33F body, had entered service in October 1979 but, from January 1981 until April 1986, had its Voith gearbox replaced by a Maxwell four-speed automatic one. The bus is working on the 75 service to Beaumont Leys and is negotiating the traffic island in Belgrave Gate, having travelled along Charles Street from where the Renault 12 saloon car is emerging. To the left of 250, a Midland Fox Leyland National speeds past the job centre as it travels into Charles Street. In the distance, at the far end of Lower Hill Street, is the Lee Circle car park. It was the first automatic multi-storey car park in Europe, and it also housed the first Tesco supermarket outside of London, which was, at the time, the largest in the UK. A total of 371 Dennis Dominators were bodied by East Lancs between 1977 and 1996, when production ended. They must have been successful, as the last Leicester Dennis Dominators to survive in service lasted until 2005. 240 (FUT 240V), from this batch, has survived into preservation, having been latterly used as a driver-training vehicle by First as their 90257. (A .J .Douglas)

227 (MUT 227V)

Above: Travelling out of Leicester along Humberstone Road and approaching the junction with Overton Road is 227 (MUT 227V). This junction was in the valley of Willow Brook, and the bus had descended the 50-foot drop from the distant Spinney Hill Road. This was the second of the five Dennis Dominator DD120s with Marshall H43/33F bodies delivered in August 1980, and was intended to be registered KBC 227V. It entered service on 7 August but, three weeks later, it was taken out of service and covered in a stick-on all-over advertisement for the Home Life Exhibition from 3–13 September. Most of this was removed before the bus re-entered revenue service in September 1980. The bus is working on the 61 service on 21 April 1984 and is passing the large bay-windowed late-Victorian villas. (A. P. Newland)

254 (MUT 254W)

Above: The new 1984 livery of red, white and grey suited the East Lancs bodies on the Dennis Dominator DD120s; it was very attractive, as it helped to break up the somewhat 'boxy' body design. 254 (MUT 254W) is standing at the bus shelter in Humberstone Gate outside the M&B Champion public house. On the other side of the distant Yeoman Street is the Old Black Lion pub. The bus is working on the 35 service to Saffron Cross Roads. 254 entered service in March 1981 as one of a batch of fourteen buses, which were the first to have the plain front dome rather than the earlier peaked version. (D. R. Harvey Collection)

251 (MUT 251W)

Opposite below: 251 (MUT 251W), a Dennis Dominator DD120 with an East Lancs H43/33F body, had the distinction of being exhibited at the Commercial Motor Show at the National Exhibition Centre in October 1980 before entering service in November 1980. The bus was again chosen to represent LCT as, in December 1985, it was repainted in the 1901 horse tram livery in order to celebrate the eighty-fifth anniversary of municipal public transport in Leicester. It reverted to the standard fleet livery during August 1987. 251, wearing the elaborate 1901 horse tram livery, is in Charles Street when loading up with passengers on the 38 service to Eyes Monsell during 1986. (D. R. Harvey Collection)

43 (TBC 43X)

Above: Travelling along Aylestone Road is Citybus 43 (TBC 43X) on 15 May 1993. The bus is working on the 35 route to the Saffron Cross Roads. The bus is a Dennis Dominator DDA142 with an East Lancs H43/33F body dating from December 1981, and was one of only nine in the batch to be fitted with a Voith three-speed gearbox. It is crossing the junction with Freemen's Common Road. The bus is in the maroon-and-cream livery of CityBus, and is being followed by a Ford Fiesta and, in the distance, one of Midland Fox's former London Transport DMS Daimler Fleetlines, with its all-yellow painted front. Overtaking the bus is an Austin Montego Estate car, distinguishable by the roof rails. (A. P. Newland)

51 (TBC 51X)

Above: Standing in Abbey Park Road Garage on 26 December 1987 are three Dennis Dominators with East Lancs bodies. On the left is 51 (TBC 51X), which entered service in October 1981; it is pictured here in the 1984 red, white and grey livery, but with only the word 'Leicester' remaining below the upper saloon windows, as soon the displayed fleet name would be just 'CityBus'. Alongside it is 70 (AUT 70Y), another East Lancs-bodied Dennis Dominator DDA160, but dating from February 1983. Both these buses have the later style of front dome, whereas the distant bus, 202 (YRT 202T), has the earlier peaked front dome. Behind the pair of Dominators is the six-wheeled Mercedes-Benz 0317, with a Ludewig half-decker RB52T body from Leicester's twin city of Krefeld in what was, at the time, West Germany. Originally registered KR-2D 61, it was a gift to the city in 1978 as part of an exchange with 85 (85 HBC), one of the 1964 East Lancs-bodied Leyland Titan PD3A/1s. (D. R. Harvey)

205 (NFP 205W)

Opposite above: The chassis of what will become Leicester's 205 is parked outside Abbey Park Road Garage on 17 December 1979. The chassis number is DDA 131/230 and, with 206, was the only Dominator delivered to Leicester built with air suspension. The chassis number consisted of DD for Dennis Dominator, while the A shows that it had air suspension. The next number is for the batch purchased by a specific operator while the last three numbers are the actual number of the chassis. Without a body, the bare frame reveals the low longitudinal members allowing for an easy access two-step entrance and swept-up chassis over both axles. Between the uplifted rear chassis members was a drop centre double reduction axle, while behind is the engine bustle, designed specifically to be part of the body structure, concealing the Gardner 6LXB 10.45-litre engine. The bus chassis had been driven from Guildford by a hardy soul who sat unprotected, save for a screen of cardboard and newspaper, on a crude wooden chair. The complete bus would return from the Blackburn factory of the East Lancashire Coachbuilders entering service in August 1980 and, although intended to be registered GBC 205V, it entered service as NFP 205W. (M. W. Greenwood)

57 (VAY 57X)

Above: Turning right from London Road, near to the top of the climb up from the railway station into University Road, is the nearly empty 57 (VAY 57X), on a journey to pick up a new duties. The original late-nineteenth-century housing, built in the then-newly developed, prestigious London Road area, had already been subjected to redevelopment, with somewhat anachronistic-looking modern buildings by the early 1980s. This type of redevelopment was stopped soon after, allowing for the refurbishment and gentrification of London Road's remaining original Victorian premises. This was the first of three Dennis Dominator DD155s with East Lancs H43/33F bodywork, which entered service in March 1982, to be allocated VAY registration letters. (D. R. Harvey Collection)

32 (AUT 32Y)

Opposite: The historic Leicestershire market town of Market Bosworth was served by Gibson Brothers of Barlestone with a direct bus service to Leicester. The company was originally taken over by LCT in August 1979 as a distinctly independent operation but, on 8 October 1982, the whole Gibson operation was integrated into Leicester City Transport. 32 (AUT 32Y) is a MCW Metrobus DR102/35, fitted unusually with an Alexander H45/33F body. It is parked at the bus stop in front of the war memorial in the Market Square. It is Tuesday 29 March 1983, and 32 is about to leave on its first day of service when working on the 123 service to Leicester via Barlestone, the former home of Gibson Brothers. (M. W. Greenwood)

65 (XJF 65Y)

Travelling towards the railway bridge over Humberstone Road as it goes into the City is 65, (XJF 65Y). This East Lancs-bodied Dennis Dominator DDA 155 had entered service in October 1982. Here it is in Leicester City Bus livery as it works on the 24 route on 8 October 1986, by which time it was just four years old. Leicester was, under the stewardship of general manager Geoffrey Hilditch, an enthusiastic operator of its large fleet of Dominators, which, for a twelve-year period from 1977 until 1989, was their standard double-decker bus. 65 has left the distant junction with Spinney Hill Road, along with the tall row of late Victorian buildings on the north side of Humberstone Road, and is passing Walker's timber yard. This was one of the few commercial remnants of the old Midland Railway's Humberstone Road railway station. The station had opened in 1875 and closed in 1968. (A. P. Newland)

78 (A78 FRY)

Parked in one of the bus layover bays in the central reservation of Humberstone Gate, and ready to turn back towards Charles Street, is Dennis Dominator 78 (A78 FRY), designated DDA168/682 by Dennis. This translates as a Dennis Dominator with air suspension and the chassis number 682, from the 168 batch of four chassis unique to Leicester City bus. It is painted in the maroon, grey and white livery adopted by City Bus in September 1984. These East Lancs-bodied buses were among the last to be delivered to LCT to this design, having been in production since 1963 and built on virtually every type of rear-engined chassis. Behind the bus is St James Street, which, by the late 1980s, had acquired a pool hall in part of the late-Victorian former industrial premises. Visible in the ceiling of the bus is the translucent roof panel, which, if kept clean and in pristine condition, helped to brighten the area above the staircase. (D. R. Harvey Collection)

81 (B81 MJF)

Loading up beneath the Haymarket Centre pedestrian bridge over Humberstone Gate in March 1985 is 81 (B81 MJF), the first of Leicester City Bus's Dennis Dominators with the restyled East Lancs H43/33F body. This body was a four-bay structure, with angled upper saloon front-side windows; a single curved upper saloon front window; and, overall, a much more angular, slab-sided design. This bus was exhibited at the Commercial Motor Show at the National Exhibition Centre in October 1984, before entering service in Leicester in January 1985. This bus was fitted with the usual Gardner 6LXB 10.45-litre engine, as opposed to the two previous buses, which were fitted experimentally with Gardner 5LXCT 8.7-litre units. The bus is working on the 21 service to Rushey Mead in the north of the city. As a comparison, behind 81 is 61 (XJF 61Y), which had the earlier style of East Lancs body. (D. R. Harvey)

86 (B86 MRY)

Diverted in November 1984 from South Yorkshire PTE after delivery to Sheffield were three Dennis Dominators. These were in exchange for three Dennis Dorchester single-deck chassis ordered by Leicester; these became 75 to 77 in the PTE fleet, having received Plaxton C44FT coach bodies on the underfloor-engined chassis. The transferred buses were Dominator DDA901s, with Alexander-style bodies built by East Lancs as their E type with a H46/33F seating layout. The bus is working on the 24 route to the Goodwood housing estate between Evington and Uppingham Road, and is painted in the 1984 City Bus maroon, grey and white livery. (D. R. Harvey Collection)

100 (C100 UBC)

Leaving the Imperial War Museum's Duxford Aerodrome site on 27 September 2009, after that year's Showbus Rally, is the then-recently preserved 100 (C100 UBC). It is still in the Warrington Borough Council livery as their fleet number 150. This Dennis Dominator DDA 1010 had an East Lancs H46/33F, and was new to Leicester Citybus in July 1986. It was one of a batch of four Dominators with the new-style, sloping front-end East Lancashire bodywork. They were trialled against 110 to 113, which had similar-looking East Lancs bodies, but were mounted on Scania N112DR chassis, which were also delivered in July 1986. 100 had a very short service life with Leicester Citybus and was withdrawn in 1989, whereupon it was sold with the other three to Warrington Borough Transport in March 1989. It was finally withdrawn in July 2009. 100 was bought for preservation and returned to Leicester in 2009. (D. R. Harvey)

113 (C113 UBC)

Four Scania N112DRBs with East Lancs H46/31F bodywork were purchased in July 1986 in order to compare them with the contemporary Dennis Dominators. Externally, the Scanias looked very similar, although the bottom of the lower saloon windows was slightly higher. After only a few years at Leicester, 110 to 113 were sold as being non-standard in order to raise funds. This was to Brighton and Hove, who were already standardising on the Scania N112 type, where 113 became their 743. 113 (C113 UBC), the last of the four buses, is working a private hire for a school day out in July 1987. (M. Fenton)

87 (E87 HNR)

87 (E87 HNR) entered service in April 1988, and was part of the penultimate LCT order for thirteen Dennis Dominators, numbered 87 to 99. For the first time in the Leicester fleet, these buses had Cummins L10 10.14-litre engines rather than the Gardner 6LXB unit. The bus had the latest angular style of East Lancs H46/33F bodywork; however, despite its modern profile, the bus would eventually be eventually handicapped by legislation, as the bodywork had a two-step entrance. 87 is travelling along Gravel Street when leaving St Margaret's bus station in February 1989. It is working on the 153 service to Market Bosworth via Barlestone, a route inherited from the takeover of Gibson Brothers. (D. R. Harvey)

88 (E88 HNR)

In November 1993, Leicester City Council sold its 94 per cent shareholding in Leicester CityBus to the GRT Group. The GRT Group merged with Badgerline to form FirstBus on 15 June 1995 and the operation was rebranded as First Leicester. The old Leicester City Bus livery was soon replaced by new First Bus flying F logo. This was before the new white, pink and blue corporate 'Barbie' livery was introduced. Former LCT 88 (E 88 HNR) is in the First all-over white interim livery, with maroon skirts and upper deck roof, which was a historical reference to the erstwhile municipal colours. The bus, renumbered by First as 39088, is working on the 12 route and is in Humberstone Gate, outside Sainsbury's supermarket, on 28 July 2004. In the distance is one of First's later Alexander-bodied Volvo B7TLs. (A. P. Newland)

152 (F152 MBC)

On 9 October 1993, just before the municipal undertaking was sold to the GRT Group, 152 (F152 MBC) travels along Melton Road through Syston towards Leicester city centre when working on the 204 route. The bus is beginning the climb to the bridge over the Midland main line railway. It is passing the entrance to Syston railway station, originally opened on 5 May 1840 as a minor intermediate station on the Midland Counties Railway line. This is now also part of the Ivanhoe line to both Nottingham via Loughborough and to Peterborough via Melton Mowbray. The bus is almost opposite the early-Victorian Midland Railway public house. This bus was the last of the 141 to 152 batch of Dennis Dominator DDA 1024s with East Lancs H46/33F bodywork, and it entered service in April 1989. This made it the final Dominator bought by the undertaking, as well as the final double-decker purchased by Leicester CityBus. (A. P. Newland)

Last Single-Deckers and Minibuses

320 (YAY 20Y)

Pulling across the road to the offside lane of the dual carriageway in Colchester Road is 320 (YAY 20Y). Originally numbered 20 when new in October 1982, it was renumbered as 320 in November 1983. Only eighty-seven Dennis Lancet SDs of these vertical underfloor-engined buses were ever built. 320 was the first of three buses for LCT, and all were equipped with Duple DP31DL bodies. In the centre of the bus's nearside is a door with a wheelchair lift and, as a result, the three buses were rarely used on bus work. 320 is working on the 17 route to Braunstone on 7 February 1987. This was just three weeks before it was taken out of service, and only four months before it and 322 were sold to Glamorgan CC social services department in Cardiff. (A. P. Newland)

96 (A96 FRY)

The Dennis Falcon H chassis had a Gardner 6HLXB 10.45-litre rear-mounted underfloor-engine and a front-mounted radiator. The Falcon H chassis was specifically built for bus work, and the Duple B52F body fitted to 96 (A96 FRY) produced a well-balanced, purposeful-looking single-decker. 96 is working on the 19 route to Winstanley Drive on the western side of the city. 96 was the last of three Falcon Hs delivered to Leicester City Transport in March 1984, but was sold to Thamesdown Transport in Swindon, becoming their fleet number 16 in October 1986. It is loading up with passengers in Humberstone Gate when still new in 1984. (R. H. G. Simpson)

615 (H615 EJF)

Working on the 21 route in the Rushey Mead 1970s housing estate to the north side of the city is 615 (H615 EJF). On 13 March 1993, 615 is travelling along Gleneagles Avenue towards the city centre. This East Lancs B48F-bodied Dennis Falcon H was one of nine delivered in 1991 and 1992 with this manufacturer's bodywork, during the brief revival of the model between 1988 and 1993. During this period, just fifty-four chassis were produced and Leicester City Bus received sixteen of them, of which nine were built with this style of East Lancs B48F body, while the last seven had Northern Counties B48F bodies. (A. P. Newland)

704 (F704 MBC)

Parked on the forecourt of Abbey Park Road Garage is 704 (F704 MBC). This was the first of eight Iveco 49.10s with Birmingham-built Carlyle Dailybus B25F bodies delivered to Leicester Citybus in August 1988, at a time when the municipal operation was under a considerable amount of pressure. Financial constraints (in part due to loss of passengers), a somewhat uncertain municipal managerial direction and competition from Midland Red East, who had rebranded themselves as Midland Fox, resulted in Citybus opting to go down the large minibus route in order to compete with Midland Fox's Fox Cub fleet. The Ivecos had a somewhat larger capacity than their red rivals, but they began the slow spiral downwards before the whole operation was disposed of by Leicester Corporation to Grampian Regional Transport in November 1993. (D. R. Harvey Collection)

725 (F725 PFP)

The policy of LCT, in an attempt to stave off mounting losses, was to open up new routes using minibuses. Midland Fox had already successfully trialled a number of minibus services, which were one-man operated and had nippy, small-capacity vehicles; consequently, they were ideal to operate in areas that previously were not served by public transport. LCT soon adopted the same policy and began running services into housing estates that would not warrant a service with a full-sized bus. In the last few years prior to its sale, LCT purchased thirty-seven Iveco 49.10 minibuses with Carlyle Dailybus B25F bodywork, and fifteen Renault-Dodge S56s with Northern Counties B25F bodies. 725 (F725 PFP), one of the dozen Iveco 49.10s purchased in March 1989, is in a queue of traffic in Charles Street in February 1989. It is working on the 32 service and is in the livery of the Little CityBuses. (D. R. Harvey)

762 (D320 DEF)

Travelling along Burleys Way alongside St Margaret's bus station, and about to turn right into St Margaret's Way, is 762 (D320 DEF). In the Citybus minibus livery, this Dodge S56 van chassis had a Northern Counties B22F body and was new to Cleveland Transit as their fleet number 320. The seating capacity of these minibuses was not much less than the Guy B's of 1927, but these small buses tended to be known as 'bread vans', a sobriquet that reflected their ride and passenger comfort. 762 and 763 were the last buses acquired by the successors to the once-proud municipal fleet and, even these in the financially stricken last years of operation, were second hand. A sad end! (D. Beardmore)

Coach Fleet

10 (KAY 10N)

Leicester City Transport's first coach was purchased in July 1975. This was a Ford R1114 with a Duple C49F body, which became 10 (KAY 10N). The Ford R1114 was 11 metres long and fitted with a Ford 5.9-litre turbocharged 140-bhp front-mounted engine, coupled to a six-speed synchromesh gearbox. The Ford 1114 was a lightweight chassis, which competed with the contemporary Bedford Y-series coach chassis. The Duple Dominant I coach body was an all-steel structure, with quite a large amount of chromed trim, and was in production between 1972 and 1976. 10 was fitted with jack-knife bus doors in order to qualify for the bus grant. The coach had three seasons with LCT before being sold in October 1978, having been replaced by a pair of Plaxton-bodied Leyland Leopards registered YRY 7–8T. (D. R. Harvey Collection)

9 (VUB 394H)

In January 1976, a pair of coaches, new to the long-established operator Wallace Arnold of Leeds, were purchased from Smith's of Shenington in Warwickshire. These were both Leyland Leopard PSU3A/4Rs; they had Plaxton Panorama Elite C53F bodies and dated from April and May 1970 respectively. 9 (VUB 394H) is parked in Gravel Street, alongside Midland Red's Sandacre bus garage behind St Margaret's bus station, prior to operating on a County Travel/ Gibson service to Anstey, Woodhouse Eaves and Loughborough. 9's twin was 11 (VUB 404H). 9 was one of the longest serving of LCT coach fleet and was not withdrawn until March 1984. (D. R. Harvey Collection)

13 (PJF 13R)

13 (PJF 13R) was a Leyland Leopard PSU3D/4R with a Willowbrook 008 Spacecar C53F body, which was down-seated to C49F not long after it entered service. Although distinctly different from other manufacturer's coach bodies, the Spacecar body was somewhat poorly constructed, and only ninety-three were ever built. Those, like the four purchased by LCT, lasted with the undertaking from November 1976 until June 1985; however, this was due in part to those on the heavyweight Leopard chassis being slightly more substantial than others built on Bedford or Ford lightweight chassis. On the last Monday of operation of the 44 route, PJF 13R is in Shady Lane, Evington on 3 September 1979. (A. P. Newland)

10 (OUT 10W)

Above: 10 (OUT 10W) was a Leyland Leopard PSU3E/4R with a Duple Dominant II C53F body which, when fitted to a heavyweight underfloor-engined chassis, was lower than when mounted on a lightweight chassis, such as LCT's previous number 10 (KAY 10N), the Ford R1114. The Dominant II had a deeper windscreen than the previous model. OUT 10W was delivered on 22 January 1981 and had a semi-automatic Pneumocyclic gearbox, coupled to an 11.1-litre 0.680 engine. The coach remained in service with LCT until May 1985. It is on a private-hire duty and is already well loaded up with passengers waiting to start their journey back home. (R. H. G. Simpson)

18 (BUT 18Y)

Opposite below: Leicester bought a pair of their own Leyland Tiger TRCTL11/2Rs in June 1983. By 1983, Leicester City Transport had graduated to the new Leyland Tiger chassis, which was more powerful than the well known Leopard model, which after over twenty years of production (albeit modified over the years) was beginning to show its age – particularly in comparison to the imported Volvo B10M chassis. They had Plaxton Paramount Express C53F bodywork designed by Ogle Design, and this new body first appeared at the 1982 British Motor Show. 18 (BUT 18Y) is working on one of the City Flyer routes. This was operated between Dover, Maidstone, Leicester, Burnley and Morecambe, with inputs variously by the local authorities at Burnley & Pendle, Leicester and Maidstone subsequently joined by Brighton, Southend and the Heysham-based Lonsdale Coaches. On a sunny summer's day, 18 (BUT 18Y) is having a break on a Blackpool service. (R. H. G. Simpson)

2 (TBC 2X)

Above: Former Gibson of Barlestone coach TBC 2X was one of thirteen coaches taken over on 8 October 1982. There was a pair of these Leyland Leopard PSU3F/4Rs with Plaxton Panorama V C53F bodywork. These were delivered on 13 October 1981, after Gibson's had ceased to be independent, being controlled instead by Leicester City Transport after August 1979. 2 (TBC 2X), with Gibson fleet names, was fitted with jack-knife doors in order to be able to operate the rural service out into the Leicestershire countryside. The coach is turning from Horsefair Street into Gallowtree Gate in front of the National Westminster Bank when working on the Ibstock 122 service in October 1984. (A. J. Douglas)

17 (YJF 17Y)

Above: Parked in front of De Montfort Hall on 14 May 1983 is 17 (YJF 17Y), a Leyland Tiger TRCTL11/2R with a Plaxton Supreme V C53F body. It was delivered to LCT on 17 October 1982and was equipped with bus-type doors and mounting points for a driver-operated ticket machine in orderto comply with the regulations under the terms of the government's Bus Grant Scheme. This included a 50 per cent grant on new vehicles. De Montfort Hall, with its impressive doric-style pillars, was built by Leicester Corporation in the early twentieth century and was finished in 1913 at a cost of £21,000 and had an auditorium capacity of around 2,000. (M. W. Greenwood)

25 (BUT 25Y)

Above: In June 1983, three of the fairly uncommon Dennis Dorchester SDA801 chassis were delivered to Leicester City Transport. All but five of the 167 Dorchesters that were constructed were fitted with coach bodies, with the LCT ones having Plaxton Paramount 3200 coachwork with a C49F seating layout. The Paramount was developed from a design drawn up by consultants Ogle. It was clean lined, with a somewhat square appearance that featured a distinctive 'feature window' just behind the front-wheel arch. The Dennis Dorchester was a mid-engined, heavy-duty, single-deck coach and was fitted with a horizontal Gardner 6LXCT 10.45-litre engine. The last of the trio was 25 (BUT 25Y) and, when it was brand new, the coach attended a bus rally held at the civic centre in Cardiff in 1983. The three Dennis coaches had a short life with LCT, as they were sold in February 1985 to Hull City Transport, with 25 becoming their fleet number 43. These coaches were used on the City Flyer routes jointly operated between Dover, Maidstone, Leicester, Burnley and Morecambe with Burnley & Pendle, Leicester and Maidstone, who were subsequently joined by Brighton, Southend and the Heysham-based Lonsdale Coaches. (D. R. Harvey Collection)

21 (A21 GBC)

Opposite below: 21 (A21 GBC) was the middle one of a trio of Tiger TRCTL11/3R chassis with the angular-styled Plaxton Paramount Express C57F body. The Express body featured a wider entrance and two-piece door, in order to comply with the bus-grant regulations, which required such vehicles to be able to work as one-man buses. These three coaches were painted in LCT livery for the 1984 summer season when they were new in the winter of 1983. 21, which had entered service on 2 December 1983, is in the coach park at Weston-Super-Mare on a day excursion on Whit Monday, May 1987. This was a typical British bank holiday, which started out quite well with blue skies, but gradually deteriorated. By the time for departure, the location of which was usually some distance away on the promenade, the soaked day trippers were glad to leave for home! (D. R. Harvey)

23 (B160 WRN)

23 (B160 WRN) was one of eighteen Duple Laser 2 C53F-bodied Leyland Tiger TRCTL11/3RHs delivered new to Ribble Motor Services of Preston as their 160 in February 1985. It was acquired by Leicester CityBus in March 1988, and was one of a pair bought at the same time, the other being B165 WRN, which was given the fleet number 24. These two vehicles were the last two coaches purchased by Leicester CityBus. The attractive-looking bodywork was among the last designs built by Duple but, despite appearances, they were neither very robust nor long lasting. 23 is being employed on an excursion and the driver is reading his newspaper during his long break. (K. P. Pudsey)

Leicester City Transport Bus Fleet
1924–1993

Fleet Nos	Registration Nos	Chassis	Chassis Nos	Body	Seating	Modifications/ Notes	Years In	Years Out
1-6	BC 9162-67	TSM TS6	3318/5/7/6/ 9-20	Brush	B32R	Rebodied Brush H26/26RO 1927	7/24	6/34
7-14	RY 1572-79	TSM TS6	3662/5/3-4/ 6-9	Brush	H26/ 24RO		10/25	6/34
15-18	RY 4573-76	Guy B	B22387/ 22298/ 22386/ 22296	Brush	B25F		6-7/27	12/37- 6/39
19	RY 4377	Guy CX	CX22499	Brush	H30/26R		9/27	9/39
20-29	RY 5541-50	Guy CX	CX22692/ 89-90/ 5/4/1/6/701 /697/700	Brush	H30/26R		12/27- 1/28	9/39- 12/42
30-33	RY 5551-54	Guy B	B22683/ 75/82/8	Brush	B25F		12/27	5/37- 6/39
34-39	RY 6469-74	Guy CX	CX22741/ 4/93/43/0/95	Brush	H30/26R		7-9/28	9/39- 12/42
40	WT 6436	Guy B	B1579	Guy	B24F	Ex-Rowley, Maltby, 6/28	8/24	6/31
41-43	RY 7696-8	Guy B	B22889/ 774/23261	Guy	B25F	Guy stock	2-3/29	5/35- 12/37
44-46	RY 7851-3	Guy B	B23343/ 235/75	Brush	B25F		6-7/29	6/39
47-52	RY 7854-9	Guy CX	CX23348/ 39-40/6-7/ 288	Brush	H30/26R		7-8/29	1/36- 10/42
53	JF 1529	AEC Regent 0661	06611156	Brush	H28/20R		6/31	6/49
54-57	JF 1530-33	Leyland Titan TD1	72061-4	Brush	H26/24R		6/31	3/46
58-63	JF 2705-10	Leyland Titan TD2	1221/0/2-5	Brush	H26/24R		5/32	2/46- 6/49
64-68	JF 5006-10	Leyland Titan TD3	3424-5/1/3/2	MCCW	H26/24R		12/33	6/49- 1/50
69	JF 5005	Crossley	91097	Crossley	H26/24R	Converted to breakdown lorry	11/33	6/39

Fleet Nos	Registration Nos	Chassis	Chassis Nos	Body	Seating	Modifications/ Notes	Years In	Years Out
70-89	JF 5873-92	Leyland Titan TD3	4623-4/6/5/ 9/8/30/3/1/ 27/32/4/6/5/ 78/40/39/ 41-2	MCCW	H26/24R		5-6/34	3/46/ 6/-/49- 1/50
90-99	ABC 175-184	Leyland Titan TD4c	10535/9515/ 10533-4/ 9514/ 10537/6/ 9513/ 6/10538	MCCW	H26/26R		5/36	6/50
1-10	ABC 31-8/173-4	Leyland Tiger TS7c	10542/39/ 44/0-1/3/ 9747/ 9746/8	MCCW	B34R		7-8/36	11/52- 2/58
300-311	BRY 262-273	Leyland Titan TD5c	15181-8/ 90/89/91-2	Leyland	H27/26R		11/37- 1/38	7-10/50
312-320	BRY 374-382	AEC Regent O661	06615150/ 3/8-64	NCME	H30/26R	Cancelled Cardiff order	9/37- 10/37	9/50
321-329	CBC 913-921	AEC Renown O664	0664269-77	NCME	H32/32R		2-3/39	5/55- 5/58
330-345	DBC 221-236	AEC Renown O664	0664331/46/ 35/8/4/44/36/ 3/43/1/0/32/ 45/39/42/37	MCCW	H32/32R		5-6/40	3/57- 6/58
346	DRY 323	Leyland Titan TD7	311690	Brush	H30/26R		1/42	6/57
347	DRY 324	Leyland Titan TD7	307781	Pickering	H 30/26R		5/42	2/55
211-219	DJF 324-32	AEC Regent II O661	06617518-9/ 3/21-2/5-6/ 3-4	Park Royal	H 30/26R		2-3/46	7/52- 6/59
220-228	DJF 316/5/7-23	AEC Regent II O661	06617511-2/ 5/7/4/6/20/ 31-2	Weymann	H 30/26R		1-10/46	6-7/59
232-251	DJF 333-352	Leyland Titan PD1	451826-9/35 460547-8/ 81-2/600/27/ 9/49-51/ 92-3/802-4	Leyland	H30/26R		6-12/46	10/59- 1/63
252	ERY 386	Leyland Titan PD1A	463001	Leyland	H30/26R		5/47	2/60
1-31	FBC 267-297	AEC Regent III 9612E	9612E1850- 80	MCCW	H30/26R		7-10/49	5/63 1-66- 9/66
32-65	FBC 298-331	AEC Regent III 9612E	9612E1816- 49	Brush	H30/26R		11/48- 3/49	1/64- 1/66
66-75	FBC 541-550	Daimler CVD6	15588-97	Roberts	H30/26R		7-11/49	8/61- 1/63
76-95	FBC 659-678	Daimler CVD6	15568-70/2/ 1/3-7/9-80/ 83/2/1/78/ 85-6/4/7	Willowbrook	H30/26R		11/48- 3/49	6/62- 1/63

Fleet Nos	Registration Nos	Chassis	Chassis Nos	Body	Seating	Modifications/ Notes	Years In	Years Out
96-159	FJF 135-198	Leyland Titan PD2/1	491360/4/2/ 3/453/7/4-5/ 361/456/ 6453/580/ 450/4/1/ 581-2/452/ 578-9/ 502037/6/5/ 4/121/4/0/ 2-3/86/1981/ 0/2187/9/ 280-1/3/2/ 188/323/2/ 4/71/68/7/ 70/432/4/ 369/431/3/0/ 524/2/5/3/ 646/5/7/574/ 648/4/871-2	Leyland	H30/26R		5/49- 12/50	10/67- 3/70
160	FJF 199	Leyland Titan PD2/12	502823	Leyland	H32/28R		11/50	12/69
195-200	HTT 484/6-7/ 98/502/4	AEC Regal II 0662	06624810/ 2-3/24/8/30	Weymann	B35F	Ex-Devon General SN484/6-7/ 98/502/4, 7/52	7-11/46	8/57- 3/64
191-194	OJF 191-194	Leyland Tiger Cub PSUC1/1	565542-4/ 5725	Weymann	B44F		9/56	12/69
212	SJF 212	Leyland Tiger Cub PSUC1/1T	577604	Weymann	B44F		3/58	12/69
161-163	TBC 161-163	Leyland Titan PD3/1	581024-6	Park Royal	H41/33R		6-7/58	6/74- 2/75
164-166	TBC 164-166	Leyland Titan PD3/1	58015-7	Willowbrook	H41/33R		7-8/58	2/72- 2/75
167-172	TBC 167-172	Leyland Titan PD3/1	580659/64/ 2-3/0-1	MCCW	H41/33R		5-6/58	1-2/75
173-178	UJF 173-178	Leyland Titan PD3/1	590266-7/ 72-3/8-9	MCCW	H41/33R		7/59	2/75
179-184	UJF 179-184	Daimler CSG6-30	30039-44	MCCW	H41/33R		7-8/59	5/71
213-214	VJF 213-214	AEC Bridgemaster B3RA	B3RA050-1	Park Royal	H41/31R		10/59	5/71
201-204	XRY 201-204	Leyland Titan PD3/1	592763-6	MCCW	H41/33R		3/60	2-3/75
205-208	XRY 205-208	Leyland Titan PD3/1	592755-6/ 97-8	East Lancs	H41/33R		2-3/60	1-3/75
215-219	215-219 AJF	AEC Bridgemaster B3RA	B3RA135-9	Park Royal	H41/31R		9/61	5/71
245-249	245-249 AJF	Leyland Titan PD3/1	610602-3/ 29-31	MCCW	H41/33R		9/61	3/75- 2/76

Fleet Nos	Registration Nos	Chassis	Chassis Nos	Body	Seating	Modifications/ Notes	Years In	Years Out
220-222	220-222 DRY	AEC Bridgemaster B3RA	B3RA162-4	Park Royal	H41/31R		9/62	9/71
250-255	250-255 DRY	Leyland Titan PD3A/1	621048-53	East Lancs	H41/33R		7/62	1/76-3/76
185-187	185-187 DRY	Leyland Atlantean PDR1/1	621943-5	MCCW	H43/33R		2/63	10/79
256-265	256-265 ERY	Leyland Titan PD3A/1	622493-6/ 551-2/9- 60/ 661-2	Park Royal	H41/33R		1/63	3/76-6/78
195-198	ABC 195-6B/ 197-198 GJF	AEC Reliance 4MU3RA	4MU3RA 5200-1/ 4998-9	Marshall	B54F		12/63-3/64	10/71
76-80	76-80 HBC	Leyland Titan PD3A/1	L02410-2/ 592-3	Park Royal	H41/33R		3/64	9/78
81-95	81-95 HBC	Leyland Titan PD3A/1	L025494-5/ 2660-1/ 785-6/ 913-4/40-1/ 34016-9/54-6	East Lancs	H41/33R		1-2/64	5/78-12/78
66-75	CJF 66-75C	Leyland Titan PD3A/1	L20692-3/ 856-7/77-8/ 905-8	East Lancs	H41/33R		1-3/65	9/78-4/80
188-190	DBC 188-190C	AEC Renown 3B3RA	3B3RA102-4	East Lancs	H44/31F		8/65	10/76
36-37	FJF 36-37C	AEC Renown 3B3RA	3B3RA229/34	East Lancs	H43/31R		12/65	2/76
38-45	FJF 38-45D	AEC Renown 3B3RA	3B3RA225-8/ 30-3	East Lancs	H43/31R		1-2/66	1/76
199	GBC 199D	AEC Reliance 4MU3RA	4MU3 RA6264	Marshall	B54F		5/66	10/71
46-55	GRY 46-55D	Leyland Titan PD3A/1	L44813-4/ 5042-4/ 60140-1/ 373-4/ 644	MCW	H41/33R		5-6/66	11/79-8/80
56-65	GRY 56-65D	Leyland Titan PD3A/1	L61079/283/ 391/4-400	Park Royal	H41/33R		8-9/66	5-11/80
1-5	LJF 1-5F	Bristol RESL6L	RESL-5/142-/ 8-50	ECW	B42D		10/67	11/78
16-25	LJF 16-25F	Leyland Titan PD3A/1	702272/ 346-7/607-8/ 62-3/710-2	East Lancs	H41/33R		9-10/67	10/80-10/82
26-35	LJF 26-35F	Leyland Titan PD3A/1	701355-6/ 87102/ 90-1/2136-7/ 270-1	MCW	H41/33R		12/67-1/68	2-10/82
6-8	PBC 6-8G	Bristol RELL6L	RELL-3/ 574-6	ECW	B47D		10-11/68	10/79
96-105	PBC 96-105G	Leyland Atlantean PDR1A/1	803260/2/ 83-5/357-9/ 73/5	ECW	H43/31F		12/68-1/69	6-10/81

Fleet Nos	Registration Nos	Chassis	Chassis Nos	Body	Seating	Modifications/ Notes	Years In	Years Out
106-115	PBC 106-115G	Leyland Atlantean PDR1A/1	803261/86/ 374/7-80/ 90-2	Park Royal	H43/31F		4/69	10/82-6/83
116-135	TRY 116-135H	Bristol RELL6L	RELL-3/ 922-5/33-6/ 40-5/51-6	ECW	B47D		12/69-3/70	2/80-4/81
136-147	WBC 136-147J	Scania BR111MH	541375/ 1400-10	Scania/MCW	B44D		3-5/71	8/83-10/86
148-153	WBC 148-153J	Scania BR111MH	541443-7/87	MCW	B44D, 225 B46D		5/71	8/83-12/83
209-225	ARY 209-225K	Scania BR111MH	541483/5-6/ 726-32/5/4/ 6-7/83/813-4	MCW	B44D		11/71-7/72	5/86-10/86
266-273	PJF 266-273M	Scania BR111DH	542165/ 391-3/444-7	MCW	H45/28D		4-5/74	To GRT 11/93
274-308	GJF 274-308N	Scania BR111DH	542619-20/2/ 78-9/7/80-3/ 5-7/4/89-90/ 88/91-3/ 5-701/55-9	MCW	H45/28D		1-3/75	To GRT 11/93
10	KAY 10N	Ford R1114	BCO4RC 59794	Duple	C49F		7/75	10/78
154-173	LNR 154-173P	Scania BR111DH	543597-608/ 707-14	MCW	H45/28D		2-3/76	To GRT 11/93
12-15	PJF 12-15R	Leyland Leopard PSU3D/4R	7604357-8/ 60/73	Willowbrook	C49F, 12, C53F		11/76	5/85
9/11	VUB 394/404H	Leyland Leopard PSU3A/4R	7001210/ 0733	Plaxton	C53F	Ex-Wallace Arnold, Leeds, 2/86	4-5/70	11/82-3/84
174-178	UFP 174-178S	Scania BR111DH	544626-30	MCW	H44/31F		10/78	To GRT 11/93
233	UFP 233S	Dennis Dominator DD101	102	East Lancs	H44/31F		10/77	To GRT 11/93
231-232	UFP 231-2S	Dennis Dominator DD101/A	111-2	Marshall	H44/33F		6/78	12/88-8/89
234-239	UFP 234-9S	Dennis Dominator DD101	103-6/12-4	East Lancs	H44/33F		2-5/78	To GRT 11/93
7-8	YRT 7-8T	Leyland Leopard PSU3E/4R	7802503/ 3438	Plaxton	C53F		10-11/78	5/85
188-204	YRT 188-204V	Dennis Dominator DD110	115-20/2-5/7-31/5-6	East Lancs	H44/33F		8/78-11/78	To GRT 11/93
179-187	FUT 179-187V	Dennis Dominator DD120	166-7/9-75	East Lancs	H44/33F		10/79-7/80	To GRT 11/93

Fleet Nos	Registration Nos	Chassis	Chassis Nos	Body	Seating	Modifications/ Notes	Years In	Years Out
36-39	FUT 36-39V	MCW Metrobus I DR102/14	MB5413-6	MCW	H45/27D		2/80	To GRT 11/93
240-250	FUT 240-250V	Dennis Dominator DD120	176-184/ 197-8	East Lancs	H44/33F		19/79-6/80	To GRT 11/93
10	KHB 186L	Scania BR111MH	542062	MCW	B44F	Ex-Merthyr Tydfil 186, 4/79	4/73	2/86
205-206	NFP 205W/ MUT 206W	Dennis Dominator DDA131	230/5	East Lancs	H44/33F		8-9/80	To GRT 11/93
226-230	MUT 226-230W	Dennis Dominator DD120	224-8	Marshall	H44/33F		8/80	To GRT 11/93
251-264	MUT 251-264W	Dennis Dominator DD120	241/36-40/ 2-9	East Lancs	H44/33F		11/80-3/81	To GRT 11/93
265	MUT 265W	Scania BR112DH	1801285	East Lancs	H49/37F		11/80	3/81
10	OUT 10W	Leyland Leopard PSU3E/4R	8030071	Duple	C53F		2/81	5/85
11	OUT 11W	Leyland Leopard PSU3E/4R	8030608	Plaxton	C53F		3/81	5/85
90	PJU 90W	Dennis Falcon SDA401	101	Duple	B51F		4/81	10/86
40-56	TBC 40-56X	Dennis Dominator DDA142/ DDA141/ DDA 146	339-42/4-8 349-52 386/403-4/8	East Lancs	H44/33F		10/81-3/82	To GRT 11/93
57-59	VAY 57-59X	Dennis Dominator DD155	435-7	East Lancs	H44/33F		2-3/82	To GRT 11/93
60-69	XJF 60-69Y	Dennis Dominator DD155	513-9/23-5	East Lancs	H44/33F		8-12/82	To GRT 11/93
20-22	YAY 20-22Y	Dennis Lancet SD506	108/10/4	Duple	DP31DL		10-12/82	2/87
16-17	YJF 16-17Y	Leyland Tiger TRC TL11/2R	8200956/5	Plaxton	C53F		10/82	To GRT 11/93
81-82	PNR 319-320M	Bedford YRT	DW 45048/ 0663	Plaxton	C53F	Ex-Gibson, Barlestone 8/10/82	2/74	4/83
83-84	GRY 627/626N	Bedford YRT	EW 450329 DW 457099	Plaxton	C53F	Ex-Gibson, Barlestone 8/10/82	1/75	11/83
85-87	LNR 85-87P	Bedford YMT	FW 453512/ 7/77	Plaxton	C53F	Ex-Gibson, Barlestone 8/10/82	4/76	11/83

Fleet Nos	Registration Nos	Chassis	Chassis Nos	Body	Seating	Modifications/ Notes	Years In	Years Out
5-6	FUT 5-6V	Leyland Leopard PSU3E/4R	7902745/ 2572	Plaxton	C53F	Ex-Gibson, Barlestone 8/10/82	11/79	8/86
4	KBC 4V	Leyland Leopard PSU3E/4R	8030184	Plaxton	C53F	Ex-Gibson, Barlestone 8/10/82	7/80	8/86
3	KJF 3V	Leyland Leopard PSU3E/4R	8030158	Plaxton	C53F	Ex-Gibson, Barlestone 8/10/82	7/80	8/86
1-2	TBC 1-2X	Leyland Leopard PSU3F/4R	8130445/05	Plaxton	C53F	Ex-Gibson, Barlestone 8/10/82	10/81	9/86
91-93	XJF 91-93Y	Dennis Falcon SDA 406	119/21/18	Duple	B52F		5-7/83	10/86
31-35	AUT 31-35Y	MCW Metrobus II DR102/35	MB7104-8	Alexander	H45/ 33F		3/83	To GRT 11/93
70	AUT 70Y	Dennis Dominator DDA160	574	East Lancs	H43/33F		1/83	To GRT 11/93
18-19	BUT 18-19Y	Leyland Tiger TRC TL11/2R	8300187/ 226	Plaxton	C44FT (23) C49F		6/83	To GRT 11/93
23-25	BUT 23-25Y	Dennis Dorchester SDA 801	112-4	Plaxton	C53F		6/83	2/85-2/ 86
71-78	A71-78 FRY	Dennis Dominator DDA173/ 168	675-82	East Lancs	H43/33F		12/83	To GRT 11/93
21-22	A21-22 GBC	Leyland Tiger TRC TL11/3R	8200600/3	Plaxton	C57F		12/83	To GRT 11/93
20	A420 GBC	Leyland Tiger TRC TL11/3R	8200694	Plaxton	C57F		12/83	To GRT 11/93
94-96	A94-96 FRY	Dennis Falcon SDA 412	144-5/3	Duple	B52F		2-3/84	10/86
84-86	B84-86 MRY	Dennis Dominator DDA901	721/54-5	East Lancs	H46/ 33F		11/84	To GRT 11/93
282	OUC 127R	Scania BR111DH	544006	MCCW	H43/ 29D	Ex-London Transport MD127 10/84	9/76	To GRT 11/93
149-151/ 153	OUC 113R/ KJD 225/ 251/206P	Scania BR111DH	543993/ 3628/ 812/3376	MCCW	H43/ 29D	Ex-London Transport MD 113/25/51, 12/85, MD127 10-12/84	2-10/ 76	10/ 86-2/91
152	RYG 666R	Scania BR111DH	543839	MCCW	H44/ 31F	Ex-West Yorkshire PTE 2666, 12/85	12/76 For s pares	1/86

Fleet Nos	Registration Nos	Chassis	Chassis Nos	Body	Seating	Modifications/ Notes	Years In	Years Out
79-80	B79-80 MJF	Dennis Dominator DDA1102	799/802	East Lancs	H43/ 33F		1-7/85	To GRT 11/93
81-83	B81-83 MJF	Dennis Dominator DDA1002	793/832-3	East Lancs	H43/ 33F		12/84-7/85	To GRT 11/93
84-86	B84-86 MRY	Dennis Dominator DDA901	721/54-5	East Lancs	H46/ 33F	Diverted from South Yorkshire PTE	11-12/ 84	To GRT 11/93
100-103	C100-103 UBC	Dennis Dominator DDA1010	890-3	East Lancs	H46/ 33F		7/86	2/89
110-113	C110-113 UBC	Scania N112DR	1809026-9	East Lancs	H46/ 33F		7/86	3/89
844-854	D844-854 CRY	Volkswagen LT55	HH003047/ 38/43/1/ 0935/16495/ 2/03045/ 16488-9/94	Optare	DP25F		7/87	To GRT 11/93
855-856	E855-856 ENR	Volkswagen LT55	HH021495/ 501	Optare	DP25F		9/87	To GRT 11/93
714	D714 HUA	Freight Rover 35D	256771	Optare	DP16F	Ex-Yorkshire Rider 1714, 8/87	8/86	To GRT 11/93
857-858	E857-858 GNR	Volkswagen LT55	HH003624/ 37	Optare	DP25F		1/88	To GRT 11/93
87-99	E87-99 HNR	Dennis Dominator DDA1015	932-44	East Lancs	H46/ 33F		3-6/88	To GRT 11/93
842	D728 PUJ	Volkswagen LT55	GH014318	Optare	B25F	Ex-Boulton, Cardington 3/88	9/86	11/88
843 813	C525 EWR E813 SUM	Volkswagen LT55	FH014318 JH001616	Optare	DP25F	Ex-Optare demo	5/86 8/87	11/88
23-24	B160/165 WRN	Leyland Tiger TRB TL11/3RH	8401120/45	Duple	C53F	Ex-Ribble MS 160/5, 3/88	2/85	To GRT 11/93
841	E169 XJO	Volkswagen LT55	JH001622	Optare	B25F	Ex-Luton & District 59, 4/88	11/87	To GRT 11/93
140-152	F140-152 MBC	Dennis Dominator DDA1014	987/2-6/ 8-93	East Lancs	H46/ 33F		7/89	To GRT 11/93
701-708	F701-708 MBC	Iveco 49.10	4766/811/ 72/87/5316/ 54/1/2	Carlyle	B25F		8/88	To GRT 11/93
709-710	F709-710 NJF	Iveco 49.10	5628/38	Carlyle	B25F		8/88	To GRT 11/93

Fleet Nos	Registration Nos	Chassis	Chassis Nos	Body	Seating	Modifications/ Notes	Years In	Years Out
715-726	F715-726 PFP	Iveco 49.10	9930/10292/ 4/450/2/4/ 514.8-9/ 609/729/ 797	Carlyle	B25F		3/89	To GRT 11/93*
727-737	G727-737 WJU	Iveco 49.10	13022/160/ 019/94/20-1/ 98/16/103/ 97/272	Carlyle	B25F		2/89	To GRT 11/93*
611-616	H611-616 EJF	Dennis Falcon SDA422	216-221	East Lancs	B48F		1-2/91	To GRT 11/93*
617-619	K617-619 SBC	Dennis Falcon SDA422	225-7	East Lancs	B48F		12/92	To GRT 11/93*
620-622	K620-622 SBC	Dennis Falcon SDA422	222-224	NCME	B48F		2/93	To GRT 11/93*
751-752	H751-752 ENR	Renault S56	221917/21	NCME	B25F		2/91	To GRT 11/93*
753-759	J753-759 MFP	Renault S56	LD223140/ 52/37/43/47	NCME	DP25F (753-4) B25F		2/92	To GRT 11/93*
760-761	J760-761 PAY	Renault S56		NCME	B25F		-/92	To GRT 11/93*
762-763	D320-1 DEF	Dodge S56	HD215844-5	NCME	B22F	Ex-Cleveland Transit 320-321	10/86	To GRT 11/93*

Bibliography

Creese, G., *Leicester Trams* (2000).

DB Publishing, *Images of Leicester* (1995).

FirstBus, *90 Years of Motorbuses in Leicester* (2015).

Greenwood, M. W., *Maroon to Cream* (2011).

Hilditch, G. G., *Leyland Titan PD3s of Leicester City Transport* (1982).

Hollins, P., *Transport Memories of Leicestershire* (1990).

LCT, *Fifty Years of Motorbuses 1924–1974* (1974).

PSV Circle, *Brush Coachwork Body Lists Parts 1B, 2 & 3*.

PSV Circle, *Daimler Chassis List 11304-16684* (2010).

PSV Circle, *Dennis Chassis List* (2009).

PSV Circle, *Guy Chassis List Heavy Series 22000-38437* (2013).

PSV Circle, *Leicester City Transport* (1988).

PSV Circle, *Metro-Cammell Body List 1936–1943* (1992).

Sedgwick, M., and Gillies, M., *A–Z Cars of the 1930s* (1989).

Sedgwick, M., and Gillies, M., *A–Z Cars of 1945–70* (1986).

Old Ordnance Survey Maps, Leicester, NE, NW, SE and SW. Alan Godfrey Maps, Consett.